TABLE OF CONTENT

1. *Idris Able Dream* — Pg 2
2. *Rawpa Crawpa & Tanya Stephens* — Pg 3 – 17
3. *My Covid-19 Take* — Pg 3 – 17
4. *My Thinking* — Pg 18 – 21
5. *Covid-19 Extension & My Rant* — Pg 22 - 34
6. *My Thoughts* — Pg 35 – 41
7. *Covid-19 Compensation* — Pg 42 – 43
8. *My Thoughts On What China Should Do* — Pg 43 – 44
9. *Successorship of Life* — Pg 43 – 44
10. *Black Warning* — Pg 45
11. *Jennifer Lopez Dream* — Pg 45
12. *Military Dream +* — Pg 45 – 47
13. *Donald Trump Dream* — Pg 48
14. *Tom Cruise & Ben Stiller Dream* — Pg 49
15. *Wesley Snipes Dream +* — Pg 49 – 57
16. *Dennis Rodman Dream* — Pg 58
17. *Black Female Dream* — Pg 59
18. *White People Being Judged Dream* — Pg 59 – 66
19. *Adultery * Plea to God* — Pg 59 – 66
20. *So Much Things To Say* — Pg 67 – 69
21. *Overview* — Pg 70 – 73
22. *Books By Michelle Jean 2020* — Pg 74

2020 SO FAR

In life …no, I truly don't know what to write. I am seeing so many things via my dream world as well as, seeing faces in my waking state that I do not know how I am staying sane.

I am dreaming about Idris Alba again. This time he was in space fighting. I can distinctly remember 2 round silver balls thrown on the floor. So, I do not know if he's going to be involved in a space Movie and or, another Thor Movie.

I will not chalk this dream; Idris Alba dream up to be war and or, further conflict happening in Nigeria. And I am so going to leave this dream alone. The conflicts in Nigeria is truly not my concern, it is Nigeria's concern. **As a Black Person looking in, it is amazing how many Black Lands on/in the African Continent that have become so warped and backwards.** Meaning, to the way Africa is with the different conflicts, tribal conflicts, corruption, greed, war, dysfunctional living, lack of unity, the acceptance of different cultural lies; you truly have to wonder if civilization truly started there – in Africa, or if true knowledge ever came out of Africa.

No, Africa is the hub; center of the world and or, universe, and not all life came out of Africa.

Right now, life has and have reached critical mass, and I am so not going to get into this because; I am tired of the way people think, tired of the way people; we treat each other.

Tired of the truth being covered up to please the wicked and evil of this planet.
Tired of the way we are destroying Earth.

Tired of the way people refuse to see the consequences of their negative actions.

Tired of the way everyone on Earth think God is going to swoop in and clean up our mess, and more.

People are truly not seeing what's going on around them globally. And Black People are the worst. They still live by their slave mentality. Hence, many are corrupt; tainted; infected with the different diseases of men; viruses that slow them down educationally, financially, heath wise, knowledge wise, spiritually, God wise, family wise, and more.

Therefore, the inept will forever back, and follow behind their inept Prime Ministers, and Presidents. All wen di ship a sink, dem a guh falla dem inept political leaders to their death.

Human life is in jeopardy.

Your life; each individual life here on Earth is in jeopardy, and no matter how God try to show us this, we will forever not learn; see. Some will put religion before them without realizing that; religion was designed to take all human from life; God. Thus, people will forever defend nastiness instead of doing all to keep their life clean as well as, learn the truth of life; God.

No one can clean you apart from you.

God is not going to clean up our mess for us therefore, the mess we've created here on Earth individually, and collective are killing us. See our unclean living here on Earth including the wars and conflicts designed by those who praise, and worship Death to keep all aspect of nastiness; Death here on Earth. Thus, Life and Death here on Earth.

No, I am pissed. I saw, sorry, was watching Rawpa Crawpa, and Tanya Stephens told the more than inept Prime Minister of Jamaica fi guh S**k im Madda. And yu ha di fool, fool dem wey a batty fallara a cuss har. Yes, some of the things she (Tanya Stephens) has said in the past leaves you wondering, but she is correct. You cannot keep people locked in their homes. Humans need fresh air, exercise, some need to socialize, and more. *Therefore, Covid-19 to me is more than a virus but something let loose in the air. Chemical and or, Germ Warfare. Thus, the continued blame game of lies by those who truly did this to collapse the Global Market, lock people in their homes like prisoners, make lands barren to affect our food supply, bankrupt some countries whilst killing who they want to kill at will.*

Yes, the Covid-19 crisis is getting to people, and by locking people in their homes you, are basically locking them in prison. As a government, you are taking peoples rights and freedom from them. *Therefore, every citizen of the globe have, and has every legal right and rights to sue their government for violating their basic fundamental human rights. As well as, sue them; (our government) for putting our life at risk with the different manufactured diseases, viruses, weapons, and conflict they create. As a government, you cannot lock people in their homes for something you did.*

What people truly do not realize is that; *there is more to Covid-19 than the government is saying.* I will forever say this until the truth is told.

For me, Covid-19 is an airborne virus that got out of control. Something the government sprayed in the air.

Look at your environment.

Where I am, the trees are not budding, and it's April 25, 2020. Therefore, something went wrong, and a tweaked virus was put in play to downplay what they the governments in North America did to the eco-system; environment. *There is another phase coming that has to do with our food chain including meat supply.*

China was targeted to me to slow the Chinese economy down. Crash the Chinese economy then blame them; China for Covid-19 just like they did E-Bola in Africa, AIDS in Africa.

Africans were blamed for E-Bola and AIDS. And African eating habits did come into play as well. So, it's us as people who are not thinking – being fooled by Corporate and Government lies and greed. The North; North America do design viruses; diseases that take human life. E-Bola and AIDS are made in labs in North America. Syphilis is another prime example of how wicked the White Race is as well. <u>Syphilis was designed in a laboratory that the Government of America commissioned to spread in the Black Communities of America, and I am going to go as far as Africa. And with humans knowing how evil America; the United States of America is, people still support this land, and want to be like Americans; the people who categorically hate them, and do all when it comes to viruses, chemical warfare, wars, and diseases to kill them.</u>

How the hell can you like your enemy; those who do all to take your life from you?

How the hell can you want the life of your enemy; those that do all to take your life from you?

My enemy is my enemy. My enemy isn't there to preserve me, but there to do all to destroy me. No Black Land is safe globally, and this Blacks globally can see. Thus, the truth of slavery is not being told. Everything is swept under the carpet to protect African lies; lying traditions that take life from life.

Like I've said in other books; <u>**GOD DID NOT CREATE DISEASES; MAN DID.**</u> It's humans; wicked and evil humans that create viruses, and diseases to kill. Therefore, no politician represents Life, they represent Death. Thus, Earth is the killing field for many; well the White Race literally. Many are not thinking.

The negative decisions of our political leaders do affect us the people, and the land we live in. Therefore, the sins of your political leaders do fall on land and people.

Your life hath no worth to these people; our political leaders so, they kill at will, and you the people; citizens can't do anything about it. You have to live by what they say. So yes, your political leaders do take your life, and rights to life from you.

<u>So this Covid-19 virus to me is no different from E-Bola that was designed in a lab, and brought to Africa to wipe out many in the Black Population because; **BLACKS GLOBALLY ARE TEST SUBJECTS – GUINEA PIGS FOR THOSE IN THE WHITE RACE, AND OUR GREEDY AND DECEITFUL BLACK POLITICAL LEADERS HAVE NO BALLS TO PROTECT THEIR BLACK OWN. THEY, OUR DECEITFUL AND CORRUPT BLACK LEADERS PLAY THEIR PARTS IN SACRIFICING THEIR BLACK OWN TO THE WHITE RACE; DEVILS THAT PLAY THE ROLE OF DEATH HERE ON EARTH.**</u>

Africans were blamed for E-Bola and AIDS. Just as the movie Contagion show you how Covid-19 is spread. *All in the movie Contagion is reality, it is you that is not seeing it.*

Some of the words in the movie Contagion the government use word for word. Wow.

How foolish – well it is us as humans that are foolish; not seeing what the governments, and corporations globally are doing to us.

The movie Planet of the Apes show you how E-Bola was spread, but many do not know this. (James Franco version of Planet of the Apes).

White People are great actors. Their life is an act. They have to show you their evils in their movies. It is you as people that follow this race; the White Race to your death. You refuse to see their evils; the evils of the White Race. *All when they show you their evils, it is you who refuse to see. You chalk everything up to be a movie; fiction when their fiction is real; their reality. White peoples' reality.*

Murder is murder, and this race; the White Race are murderers. No all, but the majority of them are. They have no heart because they design to kill literally, and they get away with this, yet you, the global populace cannot see this.

We as humans let this race get away with murder globally. So yes, we are to blame as humans for letting murderers into our life.

Onwards I go

MANY OF THEM; OUR BLACK POLITICAL LEADERS CONTINUALLY KISS THE ASS OF THEIR WHITE MASTERS THAT TELL THEM WHAT TO DO, WHEN TO DO IT, HOW TO DO IT, HOW TO LIVE, HOW TO KILL THEIR PEOPLE, AND MORE.

They; our Black Leaders are bitches without a backbone because; they seek acceptance from White Society without knowing that WHEN THEY; OUR BLACK LEADERS TURN FROM LIFE; THE WHITE RACE'S JOB IS TO DESTROY THEM; THE LAND AND PEOPLE OF THAT BLACK LAND; ANY LAND THAT GIVE UP LIFE FOR DEATH FOR THAT MATTER.

People still cannot learn that in order to live you have to live.

No government official hath life thus, lands, and the people of the different lands live in disarray; dysfunction. None realize the job of the White Race is not to save life, it is to kill all life including the life of Earth. Thus, every race has, and have a job to do here on

Earth. Yet, no one can see this, or know this. Many put religion, and their politicians before their life.

So yes, *many Black Leaders sell out their own people FOR MONEY; THE GREED OF THEM.* But trust me, their hell will be grave, and if I could ensure *DEATH LISTENS TO ME TO MAKE A GREATER, AND HOTTER HELL FOR THE SELL OUT BLACKS OF THE GLOBE THAT SELL THEIR PEOPLE AT WILL FOR A DOLLAR AND OR, THE DOLLAR BILL, I WILL; WOULD WITHOUT HESITATION.* Many cannot be trusted with the trust you put in them.

Many are so vile and corrupt that they cannot see their hell before them when the spirit shed the flesh, and even before the spirit shed the flesh.

There is a Spiritual Hell to pay. Thus, religion paint a rosy picture of life and many gobble up this picture without knowing that God cannot, and will never save anyone that is truly not of Life. See your Good, and Sins.

Life is worth it, yet you cannot see this.

Life is hard you are saying.

Life is not hard. Life is easy.

We are ones that make life hard.
We are the ones that make others make life hard for us.
We are the ones that say we love him her.

We are the ones that refuse to listen to God, and what God is trying to show us when it comes to him her.

We are the ones that do not know our tree of life. Our Tree of Life that God use to show us certain things.

We are the ones that say, I don't believe in dreams when God uses dreams to educate me and you.

You are the ones that refuse to take telling because despite life being hard as you say. We are the ones that do not listen to conscious music, or read truthful books that teach us/you about evil, and the evils of life. Yes, not many artists you are to listen to, nor are there many truthful books out. Many in the Music Industry must; have to bow down to evil.

Many have to make humans sacrifices, and more.

We are the ones that refuse to listen to good counsel.

We are the ones that want what the next man woman has because, what we have do not suit us; is not enough.

So yes, I know, but with me knowing, I know God and the protection of God. God will never, and would never let the Children of Life; Zion go hungry. And don't go there with look at certain lands in Africa. Those lands gave up Life, and **when you give up Life, God leave you to the God, and people you gave up life for. This many Blacks refuse to learn until this day.** However the devil use and abuse you, is up to the devil.

Now let me ask you this. *How many more of you should have to die before you learn the full and true truth?*

How many more Black Lands must burn; suffer before we as a people wake up and secure the life God has and have given us?

We were categorically told. If a man don't like you, they will give you basket fi caaye wata.

If a race and people don't like you, they will do all to hurt and kill you, and this none of you can see; **then wonder why God don't listen to some of you.**

GET OUT OF THE SYSTEMS OF LIES THAT ARE LITERALLY KILLING YOU. SECURE YOUR OWN LAND BECAUSE THE TRUMPET HAS BEEN SOUND.

Many Black Nations are riddled in debt that I have to wonder about Black Nations Globally.

Many run to the World Bank for a handout whist our enemies; those that kill us; Blacks at will own MANY ACRES OF LAND IN OUR BLACK LANDS. So now tell me, how smart are we as BLACKS WHEN WE BOW DOWN TO THE WILL OF THE WHITE RACE LIKE BITCHES WITHOUT A SAY.

Everything, yes Massa. No, you have to say yes because Massa own your ass literally.

So yes, I applaud you Tanya Stephens for telling that disgusting, inept buffoon that run Jamaica fi S**K im Madda. I truly don't like that ass wipe and trust me, I am not afraid to tell him to his face he's nothing but shit; the dung in every shithouse inna Jamaica; no, globally combined. I have absolutely no respect for this hog; demon that has and have turned his back on Jamaica, and the Jamaican People. None in office in Jamaica I have respect for because I see them. *Dem a VAMPIRE* that sell out Jamaica and yes, mi blame the dunces them that falla behind the demons of their political system to their death. Dyam falla batty them. **Dummies, Peter Tosh told you what your political leaders were all** *about in his song* <u>VAMPIRE.</u> Thus, none liked him Peter Tosh. <u>Therefore, they did all to kill him Peter Tosh, and the great Robert Nesta Marley aka, Bob Marley.</u>

See, <u>POLITICS IS DEATH. YOUR DEATH.</u>

<u>Politics is no different from Religion.</u>

<u>Politics is suffering. Your suffering, and the suffering of Earth.</u>

<u>Politicians have to kill, must kill because; POLITICIANS HAVE TO FEED DEATH. They have to send you on the BATTLEFIELD OF DEATH TO DIE – TAKE A LIFE INCLUDING YOUR LIFE.</u>

Therefore, <u>no politician can respect life. Will never respect life.</u> Nor can they; your political leaders respect your life. <u>You the citizens are their bait; live bait that they feed to Death literally.</u>

But den dem; the people of Jamaica get dem bulla with their name on it and no, not nyam but; guap dung di bulla without knowing <u>THEY WERE THE SACRIFICE TO DEATH BY THEIR POLITICAL LEADERS.</u>

<u>No wonder God deemed Jamaica unclean.</u>

Bunch of ediats that live there. JAMAICA WAS DEEMED UNCLEAN BY GOD. Fool, fool people, GOD HAS LEFT JAMAICA. UNNU DEAD. THERE IS NO SAVING GRACE FOR JAMAICA, AND THE PEOPLE OF JAMAICA. That you all can blame yourself, and your inept politicians for.

All the killings on the island is sinking the land further into hell with you the people in it. Look, many of you know the bible and Sodom and Gomorrah. <u>WELL JAMAICA IS MODERN DAY SODOM AND GOMORRAH.</u> It is you the people that has, and have left God. Did all that was, and is evil to cause Jamaica to become dirty. Yes, become Sodom and Gomorrah. Your colonized Slave Masters also ensured they made Jamaica so dirty that the Land and people cannot be saved thus, Jamaica – Port Royal was known as the wickedest place on Earth in the 1600's. The sins of Port Royal is/are still there – on the Docket of Death, because no forgiveness was given to Port Royal thus, Port Royal sank in June of 1692. Africa is no different. Many lands in Africa is/are going to find out shortly *that God is not with them. This is guaranteed thus Africa; Africans have and has strayed from life literally.*

Port Royal was a testament of how vile Jamaica was. Evil infiltrated Jamaica, and the people of Jamaica thus, many in Jamaica live for evil; do evil.

See unnu Science.

See unnu iniquity. Therefore, the devil did their job in causing many Black Nations to fall; lose their life, and place with God literally. See the false religions, and religious lies that are accepted globally.

See unnu Obeah.
See unnu Voodoo
See the feasting with the dead.

See the powda unnu sprinkle at people doorway to keep them down.

Laade don't let me talk about the animal and humans sacrifices that many in Dancehall, and Reggae including, Conscious Reggae Market make to ensure their fame, and fortune.

Don't let me talk bout di vial dem wey inna wata, plant at people gate, doorway, and more.

Laade di people dem name wey written pan parchment peapa.

Don't let me talk bout di duppy dem; dead wey sum a unnu set pan people. Not to mention the duppy dem wey some a unnu sen fi kill people.

Don't let me talk bout di bible.

Yes, I can go on because some of your political leaders if not all in office in Jamaica is apart of Lodge therefore, they have to make sacrifices unto death. And you the inept of Jamaica are their sacrifice. You the people are dying because when you are apart of any lodge, or secret society you have to kill, and some must drink blood. Some are passed around like prostitutes for the higher ups. So yes, <u>you the people of Jamaica are the passed around because, NOT ONE OF YOU VALUE YOUR LIFE.</u> So, anyone can kill at will on the island, and nothing is done about it. So, keep dying because the lots of you have and has elected <u>BLACK DEMONS TO OVERSEE YOU.</u> So, however they (your political leaders) sacrifice you; kill you, is truly up to your leaders. <u>You did not want good for yourself thus, **NONE ELECTED GOOD PEOPLE TO OVERSEE THEM.**</u>

For me, and to me, COVID-19 reminds me of the time when that thing; Seaga sprayed the Coconut Trees of the land to kill the Coconut Trees out, and the ediats of Jamaica still pose up that demon. But then, I did see his hell years before he died. Thus, <u>hell got him literally.</u>

<u>Jamaica has enemies, and right now the People of Jamaica are/is the enemy of Jamaica literally.</u>

And if I am wrong Lovey, and it's not Seaga that sprayed the Coconut trees, but Manley; do forgive me. My blood boils when I think of that thing, and how a Babylonian became a Head of State in Jamaica. But then, instead of electing good governance for self; Jamaicans elect demons to ruin their land and life.

Covid-19 also reminds me of what Mousilini however you spell this demons name did in Ethiopia. The genocide he caused in that land until this day, that sparked the people of the land to starve; die. <u>Your life means nothing to those who hate and loathe you.</u> We as citizens are the ones to give demons rights over us; our life.

<u>We know the White Race has chemicals to kill yet, people are not seeing this.</u>

You the people think this is it. There is more to come. Everything is strategically planned. Global Starvation, then there is going to be shortage of clean drinking water.

<u>Earth's population is increasing and there must be eradication of life.</u>
Earth cannot accommodate all life, therefore; some must be eradicated for others to live.

This is nothing new to me. When the White Race was/were developing in the name of Greed; none were thinking of FARMLAND AND PRESERVING FARMLAND. None were thinking of their life; spiritual life; Death once the spirit shed the flesh. There is a spiritual cost to the evil we do here on Earth but; billions do not know this, nor can billions see this – the hell they've created for self. ALL THEY (many in the White Race) THINK OF IS HOTELS; THEIR POCKET BOOK. And you the common folk cannot see this; that you are just money to/for them.

Covid-19 already spread, and there are people who know what happened, and are refusing to talk. They will be deemed whistle blowers. Some would be punished even killed. Therefore, humans have no right in society because; <u>**THE TRUTH IS FORBIDDEN.**</u>

Wow, because if all who are covering up the truth globally think they are going to escape hell, they had better think again. Yes, I am to warn all about their hell, but I truly do not know how to. Hell awaits all sinners because many of you – billions of you think your sins are forgiven, when your sins are truly not forgiven. <u>Know what forgiveness is.</u>

Onwards I go

As humans, you have to accept their lies, and live by their lies period; the lies that was given to you.

And to how wicked the Governments of North America is, <u>they are going to BLAME CHINA WHEN IT'S AMERICA</u> AND, BECAUSE CANADA IS A FRIEND TO AMERICA, CANADA IS A PART OF THE COVID-19 LIE. Every nation that SIDE WITH AMERICA IN THEIR CHEMICAL WARFARE OF WIPING LIFE OFF THE FACE OF THIS PLANET ARE TO BE BLAMED. ARE GUILTY OF GENOCIDE. Thus, <u>lands must be judged.</u>

Therefore, HELL IS OPEN FOR EVERY WHITE PERSON GLOBALLY THAT DO EVIL; LIVE TO KILL. If any of you think you can by-pass Death; your hell in hell; had truly better think again. <u>NO ONE CAN ESCAPE DEATH IF YOUR NAME IS IN THE BOOK OF DEATH.</u>

Trust me, I've seen a world without White People thus, I will forever continue to petition God; Lovey to exclude every evil White Person including family members out of Life. Evict all off the Mountain of Life no questions asked.

Covid-19 was not warranted. All the diseases and viruses this race; White Race develop in labs and manufacture, is truly not warranted period.

<u>So, as the White Race dishonour life, I ask God to void their life; White People's Life and Place with Life; God.</u>

Remember I told you in another book. *<u>Wherever you go, Death goes with you.</u>*

<u>It is a fool that think they can outsmart, and outlive Death if their name is in the Book of Death. No one can outlive Death in Death's Domain because, it's our Sins that cage us in hell; the hell we created for self.</u>

For the White Race, and those who run the globe due to Economics; <u>*WHITE COLLAR CORRUPTION, AND GREED.*</u> Their quest for Money, and political domination. Your hell is grave. All the wickedness you've done has and have been recorded therefore, *<u>the penalty associated with one sin.</u>*

Whatever your agenda is in life. As long as you have more Sin than Good, you cannot escape your judgment; hell. All you do must come back to haunt you. Death is the keeper of Death, and as long as you live to kill; then your Keeper; Death must kill you.

What humans fail to realize is that they are a selection. Meaning, as life; human life grow(s) here on Earth, the selection process begins. Meaning, **<u>those you elect to oversee you select who lives and who dies.</u>** This is evident now with Covid-19, and it's only going to get worse when food becomes scarce. Everyone has a right to live. Seniors have a right to life; live. Yet, in this pandemic, seniors are treated as crap; shit. Many have died. Remember, each day we get a little older and some live to be seniors. Therefore, some of you should not care if you end up in old age homes, and are treated like crap; shit when you get older.

Think.

Right now, you have to line up for food; groceries; your basic need. This should never be. It is humiliating, but people are not seeing it as such. Social distancing to stop the spread of Covid-19 when the damage was already done.

<u>It's not Covid-19 you should be worried about, but your evil political leaders, and corporate owners that kill you at will is who you should worry about.</u>

How many have truly died?

What makes it okay for governments, and corporations to kill?

What makes it okay for governments, and corporate owners to take my right to live; life away from me?

You may like this, but I refuse to. My life is my life, and no shithead has, or have a right to take my life from me. No government or corporate owner gave birth to me. My choice to live is my choice to live, and not yours; the government or anyone.

God did not put you the White Race, or any government official globally in charge to oversee me or anyone so, why is your life worth it alone, and not mine? What makes your life better than mine?

<u>I have self worth so do not demean me and my life come on now.</u>

It is us as citizens that are the fools that cannot gather truthfully and get these scums out of office as well as, shut these evil corporations down that feel the need to use us as test subjects. If your life is not worth it, then do you. Let them kill you, but do not complain.

If you value not yourself this is you. I just have to leave you alone.

Now Black people. It's time we stop being dependent on the different political systems of lies and corruption; deceit globally. <u>It's time you begin to live and stop dying.</u>

<u>We need to stop letting the White Race continually brainwash us, and take our true prosperity from us.</u>

<u>Look at the state of all of Africa and the Caribbean; how they've destroyed us literally, and still we do not have sense to establish our own BLACK ECONOMY</u>

<u>GLOBALLY. Therefore, Blacks Globally do not want better for self because we continually let evil; our enemies use us as fools.</u>

They've; our enemies have conditioned us to think a certain way by using God as their tool; weapon against us. Figure it out because as it is, due to them; our true enemies using us, we've; Blacks have become the brainwashed that truly have no roots left in life. We're; us as Blacks are letting our Tree of Life die. Some, their Tree of Life is dead with God. Some Blacks Lands cannot recover God and will never recover God, and this is the absolute truth.

WHITE ECONOMY IS NOT BLACK ECONOMY.
WHITE PRIVILEDGE IS NOT BLACK PRIVILEDGE.
BLACK LANDS ARE NOT WHITE LANDS.
WHITE EDUCATION IS NOT BLACK EDUCATION.
BLACK KNOWLEDGE IS NOT WHITE KNOWLEDGE.
BLACK WISDOM IS NOT WHITE WISDOM.
BLACK LIFE IS TRULY NOT WHITE LIFE.
BLACK ROOTS IS TRULY NOT WHITE ROOTS.
BLACK CULTURE IS TRULY NOT WHITE CULTURE.

<u>Therefore, Death cannot save you and will never save you.</u>

<u>Politicians do not have your best interest at heart so they kill you.</u> And do not tell me about your political leader is keeping you and your land safe. No one can keep you safe in Earth apart from you so, why are you putting your life, and trust in people that care naught for you?

If you truly cared for yourself then you would put your trust in you, and the true and living God.

I've told you, God is a great protector, and God will never ever let you starve. So, store up some of your blessings in God so that your blessings can collect interest. So, when Death pass over, Death pass you by.

Your political leader cannot save you from Death. They too must die; <u>have to die because they live for Death. Have sacrificed them self to Death literally.</u> So, save you because you are your greatest asset period. Listen, <u>God cannot save you if your name is not in the Book of Life.</u> God can only pass you by. You did not have a bank account with God, so God cannot know you.

You stored up everything with and in Death therefore, you have to go with Death. Like I tell Lovey; God, if I am the saving grace for humans; humanity, I refuse to save anyone who is wicked and evil.

Yes, the saved can save you, but I refuse to save anyone wicked or evil. When you were doing all your wrongs, you did not think of the people you were hurting, or the families you were leaving behind mother and fatherless.

What about the children you've murdered in the name of hate and religion as well as, your demented political agenda?

What gives you the right to kill?

Did not your book; so-called holy bible say, *"thou shalt not kill?"* Yet, many kill; go against the bible of Man not God, and kill.

Therefore, Life; God cannot kill. *It is man; humans that kill, and lie on God by saying God was on the Battlefield of Death killing with them.*

So how can God save you when you believe in lies when it comes to God?
Teach lies on God when it comes to Life and Death?

IF GOD WAS WITH MAN ON THE BATTLEFIELD OF DEATH. THIS WOULD MEAN GOD IS A LIAR. GOD CANNOT HONOUR HIS WORD. HE KILLS, AND IS JUST LIKE DEATH.

So, as God lie, Man lie also.
So, as God kill, Man kill also.
So, as God deceive, Man deceive also.
So, as God is dirty, Man is dirty also.
So, as God is corrupt, Man is corrupt also.

So, God cannot be trusted given the LIES OF THE WHITE RACE AND OR, AS WRITTEN BY WHITE PEOPLE IN THEIR SO-CALLED HOLY BIBLE. A book that has, and have deceived billions thus, billions have their name written in the Book of Death literally.

So, *the White Man's God cannot be the Black Man's God,* and will never ever be. *God is clean not unclean.* Therefore, the White Man's God is truly unclean; Death. Thus, the White Race give Death because they are of Death literally.

So Black People. Some of you have a square of land. Plant organic not genetically modified. God did not give us anything genetically modified to alter our body, mind, and spirit.

Nothing genetically modified is good for you.

All that is genetically modified and filled with chemicals truly go against life; **OUR LIFE, AND THE LIFE OF GOD PERIOD.**

Start planting a banana sucker.

Start planting tomatoes, cabbage, pineapple, sugar cane, yam.

Whatever you can plant to sustain you, do it. Stop depending on others to fulfill your daily needs. <u>More is going to die globally because of our demented, and spiteful political leaders, weather related issues, and corporate hogs.</u> Your life hath no worth. If it did, the different viruses and diseases they design in laboratories they would not design and implement. Nor would we as humans be destroying the environment – planet we live in.

You have a brain, see the truth. Open your damned curtain and see the outside. Evaluate your environment – surroundings.

Many lands are inhabitable due to the White Race and their chemical bullshit. **Nuclear weapons they create to kill and do kill <u>including, fight over.</u>**

Stop letting them; White People, and some of your greedy own over develop your land.

Look at the different concrete jungles you live in.
Look at the price to your life, and land.
Your mortality rate – life expectancy here on Earth due to evil.
Look at the death rate in your land.
Look at your economic growth as an individual, and as a collective.
Look at your country's national debt.

Now evaluate your debt here on Earth. Include your national debt. Now you can see some of your hell literally.

Without food, how will you survive?

<u>WHO IS PROTECTING YOUR FARMLANDS AND WATERWAYS?</u>

Do not buy into the tourist bullshit. The more tourist that come into your land is the more taxing it is on your health, your water ways, your eco system on a whole over time. Your land becomes damaged goods period. And I don't expect you to over stand damaged goods.

When tourist come into your land and whore like there is no tomorrow, your land is incurring debt, and those sins of whoredom fall on you the citizen of the land. You are taking on the debt of others.

Your lands to do not need anymore hotels, hostels, motels. Your land need(s) more land to farm organically.

How many nations are dependent on other nations for food?

How many trees are in your country?

Now take a look out your window. How many concrete homes; jungles do you see compared to trees, and land space?

Now tell me, how are you living?

Some of you need to literally stop developed nations from using your country as their garbage dump. Your country is not a wasteland.

Why take on the filth of another nation and cause your land to be riddled in garbage; debt?

What; you, and the citizens of your land is garbage so, you take on the garbage of others to become more filthy?

CLEANLINESS IS OF GOD.

So, why dirty your land with the filth of other nations?

WHY CAUSE GOD TO LEAVE OUT OF YOUR LAND?

Am I dreaming about this fight to do with farmers?

Yes. The fight is like a game.

Right now, I am tired because all I can see is death. My dream world is filled with Death. My waking state visions of faces I see is death; those on the Docket of Death. So yes, more Black People are going to die literally.

There is going to be shortage of food because we know there is/are chemicals out there that the White Race can spray in the air to kill crops. Maybe you don't know, but I know. I see things therefore these books.

FULFILLMENT TIME – Tony Tuff, and Smokie Benz

SAVE THE WORLD – Peetah Morgan Live at Reggae Jam 2010

Think. Truly think of this pandemic, and the wickedness of those who did this; causing chaos here on Earth.

If China spread/sent this virus; Covid-19 to North America; how did this virus create such an outbreak globally?

So, China sent a person to this land, and that land to infect them. Something truly do not add up for me. **Therefore, as the White Race lie on God in their so-called holy bible, they would lie on anyone to take the blame off self; them period.** *So, in all that the evil ones of this race do, I truly hope Lovey let the truth; full truth come out, and turn the lies of every evil white person back on them. Let their evils, and lies truly fall back on them, and condemn them.* Life isn't a joke. Therefore, do not play games with peoples' lives period. Do not ruin someone's economy because you do not have brains to see your own economic downfall – greed.

God did not give dominion of anyone to the White Race, or anyone. You cannot control it all because not even God control it all. Refuse to control it all because; just as there is good, there is evil.

God did not put strife amongst the different races; evil men; people did this; put strife in the hearts of men in the different races globally. Religion

Bunch of idiots that think they can dominate Earth. When you are long gone, Earth will still be here. You're dead. Earth is still alive.

In all you in the White Race did to defile humans – take them from life – life is/was being taken from you. Death must/have to preserves life thus, no evil can enter the domain of God.

Truly listen to the lyrics of Peetah Morgan's song *SAVE THE WORLD.* Trust me, tomorrow is going to be truly brutal for some globally. I know tomorrow therefore, my dreams of what's to come, and the past.

Right now, no one want a better way so, we live in lies in hope that the lies we live in is going to save us when they; our lies cannot save us.

Many say God is going to save them. But like I said earlier, if your name is not in the Book of Life, God cannot, and will never ever save you. If you do not have a Bank Account with God, how can God save you? God know you not. So truly think, and change your way of thinking.

Michelle

My dream world is still strange. I know Blacks are going to die spiritually and physically. Therefore, I truly cannot worry about the Sell Out Blacks of the Globe.

There are many things as Blacks we are not to do but we do them anyway.

And yes, Death is coming in my family again. It's a matter of when the flesh gives up the spirit and or, the spirit gives up the flesh.

I've been thinking about a lot of things lately. <u>One being the wicked and evil that think they can escape and or, by-pass death.</u>

Why live for greed?

The good of each individual is recorded as well as, the evil(s) of each individual. So, I do not know why some would think they can, or will by-pass death <u>when Earth is the containment unit; planet for Spiritual, and Physical Evil.</u>

Which planet are the wicked and evil going to escape to when there are no other planets to go to other than the Planet of Doom and Gloom as I call it; your spiritual hell?

It's amazing how we as humans do not see our surroundings. How we live.

Look at your environment.
See the trees and give thanks for the trees of life.

When all the trees of Earth is/are gone, what are humans going to do?

Our trees purify the air we breathe.
Our trees keep Earth in check; balanced.
Our trees help to cool our planet down.
Our trees are a part of human life.

As humans we need the trees, and if we continually kill the trees; what will become of humans shortly?

Well I know, but it's us as humans that do not appreciate the environment we live in.

Yes, people protest about the environment, but what is protesting doing when governments side with corporate destruction of the planet, and corporate destruction of the planet side with governmental destruction of the planet. Corporate, and Government Greed.

Human greed.

Why protest when it's we as humans that overconsume; buy into corporate, and government greed.

We talk about saving the planet. How about saving you?

How about cutting back on human consumption, and human waste?

Earth do not generate waste, humans do.

Earth do not pollute Earth. It's humans that are polluting Earth.

Planet Earth can be saved but, saving Planet Earth do not outweigh the greed of many. Therefore, Greed and Money will forever be the objective of the Greedy Few.

<u>No destruction can save Earth.</u> Destruction is just that destruction; the killing of All Life including the Life of Earth. With destruction being government, human, and corporate greed.

Earth right now is in a state of disrepair due to humans, and human greed.

We produce so much garbage that none have any viable solution to clean the planet up.

Tomorrow is there, and tomorrow is guaranteed yet; some humans take their tomorrow from them.

We as Black People truly do not listen therefore, God has left many in the Black Race behind, and rightfully so. What we as People, and Black People fail to realize is that.

"THE WHITE MAN'S FIGHT AND OR, THE FIGHT OF THE WHITE RACE IS THE FIGHT OF THE WHITE RACE, AND WE ARE NOT TO GET INVOLVED IN THEIR FIGHT."

<u>When we fight with, and for the White Race, we forfeit life.</u> All Life because, we are going against God. A race and people that do not know God; the True God of Life cannot save you. They can only kill you thus, the different religions that humans follow to take them from Life; God, and bow down to, and praise Death. Death cannot give Life. Death can only give Death.

How the White Race kill their own, and use their own to hate and kill is truly up to them. Therefore, <u>"THE WHITE MAN'S GOD IS NOT THE BLACK MAN'S GOD."</u>

When you accept and follow the ways of nastiness – that which is given to you by the White Race, you forfeit life – all life with God. This you need to know. So, stop siding with evil because you are literally killing yourself.

Listen, it is only a matter of time before <u>EARTH BECOME FULLY BANKRUPT DUE TO HUMANS.</u>

<u>The greed of many surpasses the good of all.</u>

Yes, the days are dismal. Nothing is getting better because the lockdown is worldwide. For me, **_life will never be the same, and despite this pandemic, people will not review their life and see what is happening around them._**

Humans will refuse to see that many must be eliminated. Greed did take precedence over life in developed nations including nations led by corrupt officials. So no, **_I cannot worry about how people choose to die._** _Many did choose the leaders they want to kill them in the name of the politician, and clergy they choose, and chose to oversee them._

Death is the call for many thus, many cannot see their life, and what is truly affecting them; their life. What people truly do not know is that Spiritual Evil is deadly, and Spiritual Evil do hinder you; your life.

Many truly do not know about Spiritual Evil thus, none know that Spiritual Evil can access your life, and bind your life to the life of them; that evil being. Therefore, all you do in life to benefit you fail; cannot succeed. This is the best explanation I can give because no one truly speak about Spiritual Evil. Many truly do not know how Spiritual Evil work.

Just like Physical Evil, Spiritual Evil is for a time.

People do not know what their Spiritual Evil look like. I know mine; my Spiritual Evil, and what he looks like. Hence life's a bitch when it comes to evil beings; spirits.

Separating yourself – your physical, and spiritual being from Spiritual Evil is hard. Trust me, it takes decades for some if you make it. Therefore, evil is something not easy to get rid of.

Outside is still bleak and cold.
Trees still not budding, and it's April 28, 2020.

Lulu.com on lockdown when it comes to accessing my account. They updated their system, and I cannot log in. Yes, sent them an email, and I am hoping my login issues will be solved soon.

Cannot upload THE COMPLEXITY OF LIFE – CONFUSION. *But at the time of re-editing this book, and adding more content to this book, I managed to upload The Complexity of Life – Confusion.*

Hopefully soon I will have this book up. It will be outdated but, uploaded nonetheless.

So, as the lockdown due to Covid-19 continues, stay safe and take notice of your environment, **_and ask the question why?_**

Why did Covid-19 have to be?
Why did Covid-19 have to happen?

Why do our leaders and corporate giants live to kill; create chaos in your life, and the life of others?

DEATH CANNOT OUTLIVE LIFE BECAUSE EVEN DEATH HAVE TO DIE. IT IS US AS HUMANS THAT EXTEND THE LIFE OF DEATH WITH OUR SINS.

Now ask yourself, what is your purpose in life when it comes to you, and others?

Now look around and tell me well yourself; what have you done to preserve your life, and the life of others?

Now I ask you. Where do you see yourself in life?

What purpose do you serve God; all life for that matter?
What is truth to you?

Do you have truth in you?
Do(es) life have worth to you?

What is your life worth?

And no, I will not have fillers for this book because I truly do not know where I am going with it. Right now, everything is boring for me, and I don't want to write daily, so I don't.

Need some true fun in the Sun.

Know that life hath worth.

Life hath worth to God, and Life hath worth to Death. Those who live for Death extend the Life of Death in Death's Domain. So yes, Life hath worth to Death.

Michelle

It's amazing how corrupt North American countries are especially the United States of America.

How the hell can you create a virus, bring this virus to another land, infect the people of that land, then turn around and say, you the country I infected, infected the United States of America, and the entire world.

Now let me ask you this, <u>what would China have to gain in infecting the global population?</u>

What economic sense would that make for China especially infecting Americans when China hold trillions of dollars in American Debt? By infecting the globe; world would mean economic suicide on China's part. Plus, I am sure the Two Twins; Chinese Twins of Old that hold China's Financial Security would not be pleased. They would be mad because, they did secure China's Financial Wealth; Future. This is how I know it to be, and this is how I am relating it back to you.

China own the Global Marketplace in product and services. So why would they crash their own economy, and the world's economy to lose it all literally? Yes, many things are hidden when it comes to the Government of China, but it's their right. <u>And yes, I am being barred from seeing into China spiritually.</u>

<u>So basically, America is saying to me and the world. I infected your land, be grateful I infected your land and killing some of your people. Now here's my bill for killing the lots of you.</u>

How pathetic and disgraceful. People and or, lands are to pay you for killing them; bringing your shit of crap in their land then turn around, and kiss your ass for the destruction you've created. Pathetic on all levels. **No, every nation should launch a class action lawsuit against the United States of America and Canada for genocide; the killing of humans, and the trees.** Like I've said, there is more to Covid-19 than it seems. The trees are not blooming therefore, it is something Canada and America; the United States of America did to the air we breathe. Therefore, our global food supply will be affected tremendously.

I do not know how true it is, but if I saw correctly; they want to make humans take this mandatory vaccine for this virus – Covid-19. I could be wrong but, if I am not wrong. *<u>Who the hell are these people; government leaders, and pharmaceutical monsters that prey on, and off people think they are?</u>*

<u>I do not have to take your mandatory crap of shit of vaccine. Wasn't putting the cold virus in human bodies enough?</u>

Now you want to tag us, and kill us even more.

Who the hell do you want to chip; microchip?

Chip the stupid; inept Blacks that believe, buy into, and gobble up your lies of shit. They have no value in the Black Communities globally anyway. See the different strains of Emphysema.

As for me, do not violate my fundamental human rights because you are not my mother or father, nor are you God. You did not F**king put me on this Earth.

You did not shag my mother to get me so F**k Off. Have you not killed humans enough?

Have you not violated our rights; the rights of humans, the rights of Life; God, the rights of the Trees of Life, the rights of the environment to live here on Earth enough?

You don't F**king choose Death for me. I have a choice, and that choice is life; to live without you infecting me with your diseases as well as, interfering in my right and rights to life; live.

You're f**king pathetic the lots of you globally.

Do not chip me with your mandatory bullshit. Stop violating me and my rights. Humans cannot violate your laws yet, you violate our law and laws when it comes to our right to life; live.

You have no right to select who lives and who dies. *God did not put the WHITE MAN/WHITE RACE ON EARTH PERIOD TO KILL ANYONE, OR VIOLATE ANYONE'S RIGHT TO LIVE FREE.*

Nor did God tell humans to be fruitful, and multiply as stated in your so-called holy bible. Death need humans to multiply – sin so that the life of Death can be extended in the World and or, the Domain of Death. You all know this thus, you use your pathetic crap of shit called the holy bible to lie, deceive, and kill. You all know your worth with Death, *BUT VIRTUALLY ALL OF YOU HAVE NO WORTH WITH GOD; LIFE.* Thus, you use religion to corrupt globally; take humans from Life; God so that they; humans will bow down to Death; all the filth we put into Hell; the Realms of Death.

You create strife with other nations.
Make war with other nations.

Go into the lands of other nations and kill thus, causing the people of that land to forfeit Life; God literally. Thus, many lands have to face Death literally. Africa, and Jamaica (but Jamaica I blame on Jamaicans) is a testament of how you've destroyed many countries, and the people of that land with your religious, and war bullshit, and Blacks are so stupid and ignorant we cannot see this, thus; Blacks fight each other like hogs for a place in hell with death literally.

<u>And we as stupid citizens; people of the globe cannot see our life is being violated globally by power hungry corrupt anal holes that have no worth, or self worth in life. All they do is live to kill, and do kill.</u>

Then you have curse of crap using religion as a by. When did God become the shit of life for anyone including religion, and religious lies?

If your life have/has no meaning or self worth to you that's fine, but do not violate my space and right to life. Do not violate the space of Life; God either.

The mess on Earth God did not create, it is us as humans that create the mess, and messes of Earth. We are the ones to listen to devils lie to us, use us, abuse us, take our life from us literally.

<u>Politics is valuable to Death not Life.</u>
<u>Politics violate all life.</u>
<u>Politics violate God period.</u>

Politicians do violate the law and laws of Life therefore, no politician can say their name is in the Book of Life.

Only one politicians name in the entire Globe; Earth is added to the Book of life and that's because he's apart of my true saved. All others can kick rocks literally.

As humans we need to wake up and see that no politician is worth it; your life.

None of you are thinking that after the flesh is gone comes your judgement, and I refuse to die in hell with any politician, any clergy member, or anyone for that matter. Death is not my choice, life is, and I refuse to hand my life over to anyone because my life is worth it, and I am more than valued to me and God for whom I call Lovey from time to time.

If you want to let your political leaders kill you, take your life from you, that is fine. That is your choice; your choice to die literally.

<u>No government, or anyone should spray chemicals in the air to kill anyone. Yes, Death must go with their wicked and evil own, but no F**KING WHITE DEMON HAVE THE RIGHT TO CHOOSE WHO LIVES, OR WHO DIES.</u>

Therefore, I am mad at God for his and her refusal to truly step aside, and walk away from this demonic race of people that care not for life. All they do is kill; live to kill <u>then expect us in the Black Race to save them. Black Jesus</u>

F them literally. You Lovey need to have self worth. When you continue to let Death; the Children and People of Death interfere in life then to me Lovey, you have no self worth, or worth. You continue to let evil use us; you, and our good and true own. This bullshit need(s) to stop, and you are not stopping this. Yes, I know you cannot come into Earth but it's time Earth do what is right, and truly evict all evil from in her. She need(s) to develop a true shield that protect her from letting evil in her.

<u>Yes Lovey, you showed me them; the White Race on your mountain but, get them the hell off.</u> These people; the White Race globally destroy life literally. They are warmongers that cannot live in peace, or true peace with anyone. Their past is Death; pure death; killing. Nothing has changed with them so, exclude this race; the White Race out of life. They cannot learn hence, their life; lifestyle, descent, heritage, culture, god, and more is based on lies, teaching lies, spreading lies, propaganda, death, and more death.

<u>*Their Sins outnumber their good yet, people still live amongst them why?*</u>

We truly need to separate from the White Race Lovey. We can no longer live with them, and amongst them. We are not hogs. You Lovey know just how nasty; filthy the hog is in the Spiritual Realm so, why are you not adhering to cleanliness, and true cleanliness here on Earth like you adhere to cleanliness, and true cleanliness in the Spiritual Realm?

When you Lovey keep our good and true own amongst this race; the White Race based on hue, and evil deeds physically and spiritually, you Lovey are violating our Fundamental Life Rights; rights to good and true life, and human rights. And Lovey, this include(s) the Black Sell Outs; All Blacks that fall under the White Banner of Death we need to separate from also. They live like hogs thus they kill their Black Own literally.

Look how many lands they've; the White Race have, and has destroyed globally Lovey?

<u>*Look how Blacks are destroying self. Stop destroying yourself. Move away from the enemies; your enemies that cause you true pain. Get the hell out of hell.*</u>

Look at the killing machines, chemicals, and nuclear weapons they; White People design and manufacture to destroy and kill, and still until this day you Lovey see with this race; the White Race; why?

Why are you backwards instead of forward; progressive Lovey come on now?

When it come to some of us Blacks you are so quick to cast lots. Meaning, cast us aside, and out of your domain yet, when it comes to White Death; the White Race no matter the hue, you have compassion for them. You do not cast them out without hesitation.

Why?

Why are you cursing self, and all Lovey?

Why lie on life period?

If you Lovey have no goodness for life and those who want and need truth; goodness and truth in life then, step aside and let someone that truly care; is truly fair and just take charge because, it's obvious you are an enemy to life; all life.

Babylon; all of Babylon is excluded out of life.

Sell Out Blacks are excluded out of Life. This is my good and true desire for all Sell Out Blacks to be excluded from Life; all life more than infinitely, and indefinitely more than forever ever without end, and it is so.

The White Race due to evil and lies against you Lovey, and all of humanity should, and must be excluded from all life also. <u>You did not hesitate to evict all of Babylon from Life so; what makes the White Race an exception to the Law, and Laws of Life?</u>

Cleanliness is not Death therefore, you Lovey; God cannot leave those who are truly trying to be clean amongst the truly unclean, and unforgiven. With unforgiven being, those void of life; all life.

Evil kill all Good Lovey and you know this.

Did you not give good, and it's man – us as humans that are killing ourselves because; all have and has forgotten what true life; You is Lovey come on now?

When you do this Lovey, ignore life; the law and laws of life, you are violating our human rights; our fundamental human rights, and basic rights, our spiritual rights as well because; you truly do not listen. Nor can you see the damage you are causing. So, if God do not listen, how can people listen?

If God have no true counsel to give, how can we as humans live good and true; clean?

Now tell me Lovey. How can anyone live clean in unclean environments?

How can we say we are clean when evil dominate Earth?

So, if evil dominate Earth, how can anyone of us say we are living clean Lovey?

You cannot leave us amongst murderers that defy all life.

You cannot leave us amongst the unclean and expect us to be clean.

Yes, it's not everyone in the White Race that kill but it might as well be, because the White Race has, and have control of Earth. And yes, this is my feel and take Lovey.

The Sell Out Blacks of the Globe that aid the White Race based on hue and kinky hair to destroy their land and people are not Blacks you know this Lovey. These people; Sell Out Blacks of the Globe are White – fall under the White Banner of Death, and you know this as well Lovey. Thus, Black and White Death – the families of Death.

People need to know the truth of Life and what constitutes Life, and Death.

Blacks are failing thus; Blacks cannot blame anyone but Blacks for our situation. We continue to choose wrong, and live wrong. **The different slaveries throughout history is a testament of our continued failure, and still we cannot learn.**

Onwards I go with this book.

If you Lovey don't care, why should we as humans care?

Grow up. Earth is dying due to over development; the greed of man; humans.

Where is the right of life here on Earth Lovey?
Where is it? Yes, I am yelling.

As Black People we are so f**king stupid that we cannot see that when we allow demons into our land, they destroy land, and people. We are causing our land and people to become unclean therefore, forfeiting life. Thus, we need to stop letting other nations use us at will.

Look at lands like Haiti, Jamaica, All the continent of Africa. No matter how You Lovey, and God show us the errors of our ways, we continue dancing with the devil whilst bringing land and people further into hell.

Look at some lands globally. *They are literal dumping grounds for so-called developed nations.* Let the developed nations keep their garbage. Let the lands of developed nations drown in their own filth. Why should your land accommodate over consumers that care not for your land and people including this planet as a whole?

You can't ship your garbage to developed nations so let these developed nations handle their own mess; garbage.

Look at how poor some of your people are; live. Your land is so poor you have to wonder if God ever blessed your lands. And we the people are to be blamed. We do not elect clean people that have our best interest at heart to oversee us. So yes, as humans; we are guilty of failing Life; our self.

Listen, Greed is not your friend.

The corrupt and evil are not your friends yet, billions refuse to see this.

<u>IF SOMEONE DO NOT LIKE YOU, THEY WILL DO ALL TO HURT AND KILL YOU PERIOD.</u>

Africa is a testament of this. Now China.

Why?

<u>Because, China is a part of Zion.</u>

All the lands, and people who fall under Zion, evil must destroy. Blacks have been destroyed; are living like, and as the destroyed. Blacks are failing thus, <u>the Successorship of Zion fall in the hands of the Chinese Nation.</u> This is how I saw it, and this is how I am relating it back to you.

The Children and People of Death know what they are doing. Zion must be destroyed by evil. Once Zion is destroyed the life of Earth – all will cease to exist, and this; billions do not know.

<u>China must be destroyed. Just as Blacks have failed; been destroyed</u> – evil have to make China fail. Thus, the Dragon giving power to Satan and or, however revelations of your bible say. But I know Revelations of man's so-called holy bible is wrong.

If China is conquered that is it for Zion. Life would have failed thus God would have failed.

<u>The United States of America is not a friend, or true friend to anyone.</u> No, they are a friend to everyone. <u>Friends are not true therefore, friends set you up, corrupt the minds of people, get people to side with them to implement unfair sanctions on lands that will not bow to their evil will, bully tactics, and corrupt ways.</u> **Friends kill you hence, there is no truth in friendship just lies. And no, I am not spreading hate. This is a fact that many cannot see because, the United States crave power thus, they bully lands, kill to have and get power. Anyone who oppose them, they set up and kill. Therefore, satisfying Death with death; all the wrongs and ills they do daily nationwide, and globally.**

Stephen Marley <u>FALSE FRIENDS.</u> Listen to the lyrics of this song. In life no one need false friends – frenemy. We need true friends that will stand by you when the going gets rough.

True friends are rare I know this. Thus, I stay away from people literally.

Listen, this world is not run with MUTURAL RESPECT for each other. You have sick ass people that develop weapons, viruses, nuclear weapons, atomic bombs, propaganda, all manner of evil to discredit you especially if you do not conform to their lies – diseases. Because lies are diseases that some strive on; tell. <u>*If you are not my enemy why the hell should I hate you?*</u>

<u>**You've done me nothing so, why should I side with others against you?**</u>

<u>**Why should I listen to any demented politician, and hate you?**</u>

<u>**Why should I listen to the sick and lying bastards of the clergy, and hate you?**</u>

<u>**Why should I listen to anyone that hate you, and side with them to hate you?**</u>

<u>Not even God is safe when it comes to lies thus, man's so-called holy bible of lies and deceit that was commissioned by King James that billions swear by, and live by.</u>

Unclean cannot be clean hence God has, and have left billions behind.

Yes, people are still searching for God yet, many cannot see that no one can find God in dirty places, and amongst dirty people.

Earth is a cesspool of Sin. So, tell me; how can you find God in Sin, and Sinful Places?

We as humans have and has condemned ourselves because we accept lies – the lies of the White Race as being true; the truth.

Now tell me, where is the truth of all Black Nations?

Where did our civility go?
Where is/are our true history; life story, and lessons?

Where are our true books that teach the truth of us; our true and good life with God?

Where is the Book of Life; Creation?

Where did that book go; the Book of Life; Creation?

<u>With evil, no one should attain Life. You must attain Death, and this is why these people; the White Race and all who fall under the White Banner of Death give you Death. THEY MUST SHED BLOOD, and get you to Sin.</u>

When they kill, and you sin reckless and rude you cannot, and will never ever attain Life; God.

Listen, the White Race live by lies; myths; all that is wrong. Therefore, they cannot give right; hath no true giving in them.

God never told me to hate you. Yes, if God has a bone to pick with a nation, I will stand firm with God and not go into that land. I refuse to.

If God say not to marry into a particular race, I have to listen to God because; God knows best. I refuse to stand with that race. *Will not marry into that race, and will commission my children not to marry into that race.*

Listen, Babylon deceived many in the Black Race thus Mother Africa is the way she is.

Many in the White Race based on hue and evil deeds did deceive many in the Black race thus, Blacks Globally are dysfunctional; cannot unite truthfully. Plus, God did show me over and over again that many in the Black Community will not listen to me.

For me it matters not if Blacks do not listen to me. *All I tell God is, leave those Blacks alone. Lock them the hell out of life period.* If they want to die with Death let them die. I refuse to save any. All it means is that; these Blacks love the abuse they receive from other nations. So, when the complaints come in, I truly hope God close off these people; those Blacks who refuse to listen to good and true counsel.

God is not there to deceive anyone despite me getting down on God.

God cannot lie despite me calling God a liar.

God cannot go where God is truly not wanted.
God cannot go anywhere unclean.

God cannot petition Death not to take you if you belong to Death. Meaning, your name is in the Book of Death due to your sins.

If you have forfeited your life with God, God cannot return your life unto you.
You've severed ties with God literally. This Ethiopians of old found out the hard way. God still has a bone to pick with Ethiopia. They were the first nation to discard life literally. Thus, I've told you in other books, *NOT ALL OF AFRICA WILL BE SAVED.*

God is no ones' bitch. Therefore, humans do not respect God on any level.

We accept the lies of the bible and say these lies are of God. Like I've said in other books.

One commandment of Moses states; **"thou shalt not kill,"** as written in man's so-called holy bible, and in my book; **RISE GOES UP** yet; **God was on the Battlefield of Death killing people with his prophets.** Thus, God cannot obey and or, keep his or her own law. God break the laws he's given unto man; humans to keep.

Now, If God was on the Battlefield of Death with his or her prophets, then God would have succumbed to Death thus, making God Death's BITCH literally.

When you accept lies like this; the lies of the Bible; the White Man's Bible, you are telling God Death is more powerful than life, and he and or, she God is a Bitch; Wimp that have to, and must bow down to Death. *We know the White Man's Bible – so called holy bible is a lie; fraud that lie on God big time.* This book is so demeaning to life; everyone on Earth yet, humans swear by the nastiness of this book. So, because you trust the White Man's Bible – so called holy book over God, God cannot save you.

God did not create humans out of incest.

The White Race push the incest agenda because absolutely no sees the truth. No one see that those who wrote the bible, keep the Scrolls of Death – the bible, preach from the bible, accept the bible, and more have no truth or cleanliness in them.

If God took a rib from Adam to create Eve. Then that would make Adam Eve's father. Therefore, father shagging daughter.

So, if man's beginning is nasty, their end must be nasty also. And this nastiness we see here on Earth.

We as humans are being used by nasty people to prolong their nasty life, and lifestyle in Death.

So, because billions accept the nastiness, and lies of the White Race, billions have, and has forfeited life literally. Thus, *"HELL IS FULL OF BLACK PEOPLE AND RECRUITING MORE."* This is how I saw it, and this is how I am relating it back to you.

So yes, Blacks do accept lies, and live by lies, and Blacks do pass these lies down to their children, thus forfeiting life with God. **See the nastiness of Religion, and the lies Religion told on God literally.**

You believe the true and living God is nasty, and that God would give you unclean things to live by. So, when you believe this nastiness of God, God cannot know you.

Yes, negative is amongst positive here on Earth, but this is Mother Earth's fault. <u>She opened up her Garden and allowed evil to come in.</u> Therefore, evil is destroying her day by day.

Earth cannot grow; expand the way she should.
Earth cannot live the way she should; clean.

Earth cannot and or, can no longer maintain evil. Evil has and have gotten way too out of control. The fact that humans are selected; who lives and who dies is truly not fair, or worth it. Yes, we as humans are to be blamed for the poor choices we make when it comes to our political leaders, clergy leaders, self, god, teachings, boyfriends, husband; spouse, and more.

<u>Let me ask you this; why is it legal for people in the army to kill, and not you the ordinary citizen?</u>

If God say Henry, I do not like killing – anyone taking a life; the life of another human. Why are humans killing?

Why are you Henry going on the Battlefield of Death and dishonouring God?

Do you not trust the lies of your political leader over God?
Do you not put politics first; before God, and your life?
Do you not side with Death over life; all life?

Yes, Henry you can argue that you are not taking a life; because you cannot kill that person's spirit.

No, you cannot Henry because God requires humans to come to him or her, the way they are. As flesh and spirit. So yes, you are taking a life. You are taking away the flesh of a human from God and more importantly, because; you've violated the "thou shalt not kill" law, you have just killed yourself physically, and spiritually. You cannot be saved by God because you broke a vital commandment willingly, and knowingly. Your name must go into the Book of Death. Your time in your hell cannot be numbered because I truly do not know the cost for Willful Sins, and Sins knowingly done.

So no, I cannot comprehend why humans would allow others to take their life from them.

Yes, I am learning the truth and it wasn't easy for God for whom I call Lovey from time to time, but; knowing what I know, I refuse to let anyone tell me to hate another person. *I do not know them; that other person so,* <u>**why should I hate them because you hate them?**</u>

My life is not your life. And, <u>***if you did not create conflict with that person, why would that person hate you?***</u> Meaning, what did that person do to you for you to hate them, and vise versa?

<u>Hate is a disease. Therefore, our political leaders globally are a disease.</u>

<u>The clergy – spiteful and deceitful demons that run the churches, mosques, synagogues globally are a disease.</u>

<u>Warlords are diseases.</u>

<u>Pirates – the pirates of death are diseases.</u>

<u>Parents that sell their children to the highest bidder are worse that shit, but they too are a disease.</u>

So yes, Earth has many mentally sick people that are truly diseased living in her. So yes, 2020 so far have, and has been messed up globally. Death rising, and people are truly dying.

Therefore, humans truly need to reflect – look into themselves, and see where their life is truly heading.

We cannot say God is our keep and defy all the laws God have and has given us because of different evil people; races here on Earth.

We know the White Man's God is truly not the Black Man's God, or anyone's god period.

We know the God and Gods of Babylon is/are not the God and Gods of the True Black Race.

We know the God and Gods of China is truly not the God and Gods of the True Black Race.

<u>Yes, the Chinese Race is a part of Zion. They are the successors of Earth once Black People Fail due to our ignorance, and stupidity.</u>

We fail to listen therefore, accepting lies, and defying life. An, wen tings don't work out fi us, we cry to God an sey life nuh fair. **<u>But, did any of you look into the wrongs you do each and every day?</u>**

<u>Did any of you look at the God you serve; choose for self and family?</u>
<u>Did any of you look at the nastiness you accept and say is of God?</u>

Look at your beliefs because; *<u>"NO BELIEF CAN GET YOU INTO GOD'S KINGDOM."</u>*

<u>YOU NEED TO KNOW.</u>

<u>KNOWLEDGE IS ONE OF THE KEYS TO LIFE.</u> So; know, and not believe.

Belief mean(s) you are unsure.
Knowledge means you know. Are rock solid, and cannot be moved.

The problem with some of us in the Black Community Globally is that wi too dyam licky, licky.

Some are so conditioned by the different religious beliefs of men that they are consumed, and wrapped up in religion that they cannot see God before them. They know not God anymore but Death.

Many, the devil offered the world and they took it without knowing that all the devil gives you must be taken away from you eventually. The devil is the true giver backer taker, and you must die because you went against life, and the cleanliness of life.

<u>ALL THE DEVIL GIVE YOU ISN'T TO SAVE YOU, IT WAS, AND IS TO KILL YOU</u> and this is what's happening here on earth.

<u>*Further, it matters not if you do business with the devil or their children. After a time, the devil will turn against you, and do all manner of evil to you.*</u> This has and have happened to Black People, and is still happening to Black People today. Now China is the target; **<u>final target</u>** of evil, and you are not seeing this. Thus, evil use Blacks at will. <u>*Therefore, Blacks are used as guinea pigs globally for the different races.*</u> We fail to realize that no one can seek acceptance from the devil if you are of Life.

<u>*The job of evil is to cause you to sin so that you forfeit life.*</u> Once you disobey God, it's God's right to take your name out of the Book of Life, and let evil have their way with you. Yes, we have Physical Life and Spiritual Life. We also have Physical and Spiritual Death with Spiritual Death being your hell. The hell you created for self here on Earth with your sins.

So yes, the devil did win over billions. Now billions must pay the price in the form of their life. Billions are going to die because, <u>*billions have no worth with God, and in God.*</u> Meaning, billions did not store up any good in God therefore, God cannot save billions. You do not have a true Bank Account, or Bank Account with God. Yes, a Life Savings Account with God.

So, if you have no savings in God, and with God; <u>*how can God truly save you, or save you?*</u>

You squandered your wealth; life with God now, you want God to loan you and or, give you life.

You're dead. Nor can God loan you life.

God cannot raise the dead, or save the dead. God can only raise up life, and save life; the good and true, and truly trying to be good of life.

Michelle

You know what is so hurtful in all of this.

<u>*Black People cannot truly, and truthfully unite Globally for our better good.*</u>

Instead of uniting and stand firm; solid with each other, <u>we cut down each other and build other nations instead of truly building our own.</u>

Everyone and anyone can go into Black Lands and rape the people and land of everything, and we are okay with this because; <u>what GOD HAS AND HAVE GIVEN US IT WORTH SHIT TO THE LOTS OF US.</u>

<u>*WE RESPECT NOT GOD THEREFORE, WE CANNOT RESPECT OUR SELF OR THE LAND WE LIVE IN.*</u>

Every nation own Black Lands; then we complain about the different nations owning us like slaves, mistreating us, and more. <u>Shut the hell up and do for your land.</u> Black Nations need to make it easier for our own Blacks to vacation in Black Lands like Africa, and the Caribbean so we can contribute financially in uplifting our economy thus, building our own in a true and positive way. But then; wi suh bad mine, we've become literal fools to the White Man's Society of Lies and Deceit.

We build other nations; why the hell can't we build ours?

Look at how much we spend on fashion – the fashion of others. We build them, then they say; dem nuh want wi fi wear dem clothes. Therefore, we need to truly support our Black Designers.

Look at how much money we spend on fake hair; haase batty. What is wrong with our own Natural Kinky hair?

Why can't we rock the perfection of more than gold God has given us to differentiate us from the different races?

Wi build foreign lands then they turn against us by using brutal force on our people. Some even tell us to get out of their country like a fi dem.

How many Black Youths are brutally killed in America; the United States of America, and other lands yearly?

Therefore, as Blacks we've forgotten our civilized way of Life to live like the dung of the earth, thus; the different nations can class us as shit, and we accept it. We refuse to build our own truthfully.

Trust me, if I truly had it to give, I would not hesitate to help the true needy dem. God know, and knows my good intention towards true giving hence, I am truly disappointed that I cannot give; build homes for some in our Black Communities Globally. But the little I give when I can it still precious to me.

Trust me, Black Lands would stay Black and no outsider can, or could come in and rape our land and people of their wealth.

Black Women and Men would respect themselves including, respect their sexuality. None can our could be bought and sold. You want to lay with our men and women, then you have to; must marry them period. And if you refuse, you will be imprisoned for more than life. No whoredom allowed. Keep your nastiness in your own land period. Blacks are not prostitutes, and service jockeys for the different nations period.

As Blacks, we need to start representing ourselves truthfully come on now. Why the hell should other nations become super rich and profitable off us; Blacks?

Think. The riches of the world isn't benefiting us as Black People because we take our wealth and give it to other nations. Why?

Why can't we have our own viable, sustainable, profitable, truly growing, and uplifting Black Economy?

Why should Black Lands be drained of their resources whilst benefiting those that do all to kill us due to hate, and jealousy?

When you talk to some; young youths, they are as backwards as they come because dem dey pan pump and pride; don't want to work but beg like dogs. This is what we've become yet, wonder why the Black Communities Globally suck; is so damned poor, and destitute.

We sell each other out.
Sacrifice each other.
Accept the lies of different nations.
Try to be like other nations instead of living as our true self.

We adopt other people's cultures, doctrines and say it is the way. Instead of looking into our past, and keeping our past; the greatness we have done, we allow others to rob us of our greatness, and say our greatness was theirs; is theirs.

Tell me something. **WHERE IS THE BLACK WAY?**

WHAT HAVE WE DONE WITH OUR SELF WORTH?

WHAT HAVE WE DONE WITH OUR SELF RESPECT?

Yes I am so sad because this is not the way things were meant to be or was, but when we give up Life for Death, Death can claim our language, culture, life, land, truth, all we've done here on Earth and Beyond and say they did it; Death did it all.

We are not appreciative of us. Therefore, the White European Agenda is pushed. <u>Well what about the BLACK EUROPEANS THAT WAS/WERE THERE IN EUROPE LONG BEFORE WHITES CAME ALONG?</u>

<u>What about OUR BLACK EUROPEAN CULTURE?</u>

<u>What about OUR BLACK EUROPEN LIFE, AND LIFESTYLE?</u>

<u>Does our culture and existence in Europe not matter?</u>

Why cast Blacks aside like we matter not?

<u>We matter, but it's us as Blacks that matter not to self, our life, our true life story, existence, True Black God.</u>

We dumb our self down to fit into their mould; the mould of White Society. <u>But what about the Black Mould?</u>

With all that is happening Globally, we as Blacks have not stepped up to Build, Create, Plant good and true so that when the worst come, we are mentally, physically, and spiritually prepared.

We have food to eat, clean drinking water to drink.

When lands are in need of food, we as Blacks supply those lands with food if we so desire. I say if we so desire because, I think about *WHAT THE WHITE RACE HAS AND HAVE DONE TO BLACKS OVER THE YEARS AND CENTURIES.*

The abuse many Blacks had to face.
The way they treat us.
The way they lie on us.
The way they lie on God.
The way they defame us as a people.
<u>The way they defame our God.</u>
Destroyed our truth.
Destroyed our life.
<u>Destroyed this planet we call home.</u>

The way they take our God from us and gave us false gods to bow down to.

Yes, there are a lot of things that bother me hence, Black Politicians are shit in my book.

Instead of Building Black Lands good and true, they; our Black Politicians destroy our land, and keep the people in abject poverty.

Black Lands are so poor that in some areas nothing grow to how dead we've become. So, as our land is poor, and void of life so are many in the Black Race.

We've adopted systems that kill us literally.

Systems that we cannot strive in. Instead of keeping our TRUE BLACK OWN, we destroy our Blackness; Truth in Life, and Truth with God literally.

We were never a poor race of people but look at us now. Begging for the scrapings off our colonized slave masters' plates globally.

Where did our Black Pride go?
Where did our true Black Building go?

But then again, not all Blacks like to see their own rise literally.

We've adopted a mentality where we have to destroy our own in order to live here on Earth which is so sad.

We even have our own sacrificing their own for riches; fame. So no, I should not worry about Blacks Globally because; we are truly not united when it comes to uplifting, and building our True Black Own. Thus, God did show me and tell me this, and still showing me, and telling me this that; Blacks will not listen to me.

Hell is real and, "HELL IS FULL OF BLACK PEOPLE, AND RECRUITING MORE."

So, despite my pain, I have to carry on. I have to build me with the little means I have. I cannot worry about the Global Affairs of humans. Right now, the selection has begun. We have people selecting who lives, and who dies. Life is meant to live not die, but you have some in Corporate America; the Corporate World including our Governments Globally that cannot live right; truly do not care about the life of their citizens. But that's fine by me because; I know hell, and some in office and the Corporate World truly do not know their hell, and the time they must spend in hell before their spirit is extinguished.

So no, I worry not about White People because; THEIR HELL IS TRULY GREAT.

For you the Black Political Leaders of the Globe. _I AM TRULY SMILING BECAUSE; THERE IS TRULY NO PARDON FOR ANY OF YOU._

Wow to your hell, and the evils you have done to hurt your land and people.

All those who aid the lots of you in killing; hurting your land and people; I am smiling because I know hell patiently awaits all. Wow to the patience of Death; those who truly own the lots of you literally.

To you the Black Politicians of the Globe that fight and keep your people and land in abject poverty.

Wow, vengeance is truly great sometimes when you know the hell of the lots of you. So yes, I am smiling because:

Every citizen you cheat, there is a price associated with your cheating.

For every life you've taken, there is a price associated with the life you've taken.

For every year you are in office living the high life whist leaving your people to sin, there is a price associated to the high life you were living.

Every sin the citizens of your land commit, there is a price associated with that sin. You are held accountable for those sins because you are Prime Minister, President, Overseer for that land, and people. So, if your people combined have and has racked up gazillion trillions and billions of sins, those sins are added unto you the Prime Minister, President, Overseer of the land. So yes, I have no need to worry about any politician or priest; clergy person because, _hell will always be glorified; meaning, be happy with the lots of you because you serve hell just fine. Yep Death is happy because; NONE OF YOU CAN TAKE YOUR NAME OUT OF THE BOOK OF DEATH LITERALLY. This you are more than guaranteed._

Your name is etched there; in the Book of Death for numberless years in hell; well your hell. You did create your own hell. _No goodness that you do can outweigh your sins literally._ And yes, if any good you do…nope, no, your sins stay because; _a lot of things you all do is willfully, and knowingly done._ So yes, Life is truly Good when it comes to locking out the demons of Earth that do for Death; a place with Death in your hell.

God is good even though I cuss out God sometimes due to anger.

And forget it. You can question God.

You have parents, what is the point of having parents if you cannot speak; talk to them; your parents?

You have issues in life, go to your parents and speak to them about these issues.

If you have good parents, why seek the help of others when your parents are there?

God is no different. Why seek the help of the clergy when you can go directly to God for all your needs and wants?

There are certain things God cannot do.
There are certain things God cannot give you.

Lord I know this for a fact; the things God cannot give you.

Like I've said in other books. Do not tell God you want a man. You will get just that anyone. This I learnt the hard way. Give God all the details; your needs and wants in the person you are looking for. So, if you need mutual respect amongst each other, tell God.

If you need him to hang – no, let me be me. If you need your man to have over six inches standing penis wise, tell God.

If you need a man that is compatible to you, tell God.
If you need an over standing man tell God.

If you need that person to be a certain colour; race tell God.

If you need a truthful man tell God. Everything you want and need in that person tell God. **_Leave nothing out._**

If you need to be in a truly committed relationship with that individual, tell God therefore, no cheating is allowed. The day you cheat on each other is the day you would have broken your vow with/to God. So do not enter a committed relationship with anyone if you know you will not last. Committing to someone with God is more scared than marriage.

Let me stop. There are many things to know. Hence humans truly need to learn how to respect each other. Yes, my values are not yours therefore, I stay away from people.

I need God in my life. I truly do not need God to come out of it; my life. Therefore, I refuse to let the White Race, or any race, or anyone play me like monopoly; their game. I know God therefore, I know life, the True Life of the True Black Race, and God. Therefore, I do not need religious lies, or systems based on failure; lies to kill me, or take me from Truth; God.

I need to live.

Although you cannot see hell there is a hell. I see into hell therefore, I know hell. Have told some of their hell in some of these books.

I know Death also.

Can, and have seen in(to) the Realm of Death.

I know what Satan look like, and have told you in some of my very earlier books what Satan look like.

I've told you about 666 in some of these books.

So strive not to go to hell – your hell because…..let me leave it alone.

We know how hot fire is. Why want to die to go to hell?

Why give up Life for Death?

Michelle

Yeah, it's May 1, 2020, and outside looks like crap – shit, and it's cold. Trees are barely budding, but I am so not worried at all.

Body in pain, and I am looking at a different sight to upload my books. I cannot deal with Lulu.com anymore. I've come to the end of my run with this company.

Writing for me now is I wouldn't say tiring, but disappointing for me. You spend thousands on books to yield no result. So yes, I am tired of my failure. Can't keep sinking money into something that has basically financially bankrupt me. Just going to write for fun; to please me and keep me going from now on.

Onwards I go with this book.

So, I was thinking. Who is going to compensate the families of the lives taken by Covid-19?

America want to hold China Accountable.
Canada want to take action against China.

And I am saying for what?

What bullshit on North America's part! How can you take action against someone for something we in the North created in labs?

AIDS, E-bola, SARS, every manmade disease; why are we as humans not charging our governments, the different so-called scientists that help corporations to develop these diseases, the corporations that pay people to kill at will for crimes against humanity; us as citizens?

How many have died due to these manmade diseases yet, our governments, these so-called scientists, these corporations go free for the crimes they commit against us as citizens of that land, and other lands.

<u>Now, how sound would China be if they created a virus to ignite death in other lands?</u>

By creating a virus and spreading this virus globally would be economic suicide for China, and the Chinese nation is not that stupid, or stupid.

I've never heard of Chinese creating strife with anyone. But then, the White Race are great liars, actors, pretenders, propaganda makers, warmongers, predators, strife loving demons that create hate, and strife everywhere they go. <u>If they can literally lie on God, they will lie on anyone to save their ass. Meaning, TAKE THE BLAME OFF THEM AND PUTTING THE BLAME ON SOMEONE ELSE.</u>

It's time we as Blacks stop building Societies of Doom with our spending, and start spending on our self physically, economically, mentally, spiritually, life wise, and more truthfully.

They; America did this shit with E-bola, SARS, and more, and people believed them; liars that destroy it all here on Earth in the name of MONEY, AND GREED.

<u>**Dyam criminals literally.**</u> Lies run White Society period. *And, if I was China; I would smile and say, you are blaming me; my country for something you brought into my land to kill my people and slow my lands economic growth, and spiritual growth down. Okay.*

You want someone to blame; blame yourself because it's you that did this, thus collapsing; destroy your environment, the economy of other lands, as well as your economy. You destroyed your people, and killed people in other lands globally.

The World Health Organization knew this so, they too must take blame for murder because; they hide the truth from the citizens of the world.

Know this. China will not take the blame for your callousness; stupidity when it comes to destroying yourself, and other nations in the name of Money and Greed. China is not your scapegoat. <u>Continue using Africa, and Caribbean lands as your scapegoat but not us.</u> Now, since you want to play your nasty games; your blame game. <u>Every cent America owes my land, I need it all within 30 days no and ifs or buts. Pay us what your land, and businesses owe to us.</u>

As for trade, I; China will be suspending trade to ALL NORTH AMERICAN LANDS. More specifically Canada, and the United States of America, and withdrawing all Chinese Civilians that are Chinese Citizens; Nationals from your lands effective immediately. China have homes they can live in free of charge if necessary.

<u>Lies on China we will not tolerated therefore, China will seek alternative routes; other trading partners that are not liars, and thieves; devils to do business with.</u>

China will clean up China and put our Chinese Nationals first. China is economically viable and sustainable therefore, it's time for China to do for China, and not the global communities of liars and deceivers.

But then, I should not worry about this. <u>Once Blacks lose Zion then China will become unstoppable globally.</u>

All that I write in regards to Death taking their wicked, and evil own. Whomever the Banner of Life fall upon in China can ask God for this; separating China from their enemies, and for China not to do any business with their enemies.

They the Carrier of Life can also petition God to take the White Race off the Mountain of Life. Yes, exclude all Whites out of Life period.

The fact is; <u>CANADA AND THE UNITED STATES OF AMERICA CANNOT STOP CHINA FROM DOMINATING THE GLOBE.</u> China and or, the Asian Race excluding Babylonian Indians that say they are Asians is next in line to succeed Black People <u>ONCE BLACKS FAIL.</u> And it's a matter of time before Blacks fail life fully. This is how I saw it, and this is how I am relating it back to you.

Life cannot give Death access to Life period. Death will never allow this because Death is not Life, Death is Death therefore, Death ensure all who have more sins than good face – see their Death; Hell.

Listen. With the way Blacks are; are going, <u>anyone can bet; put money on Life that Blacks will fail God.</u> Blacks will lose their place with God, and successorship of life must/will fall in the hands of the Chinese. It's that simple.

Many Blacks do aid the Devil in destroying their own people. Therefore, Blacks are losing their life, and place with God literally. Go back to Mama Africa and beyond Slavery. <u>Therefore, Africans need to tell the truth of why Mama Africa had to get rid of some of her evil own.</u>

Michelle

Dream world not focussed. Can't fully remember most of my dreams. I truly cannot remember if better is coming after all the craziness is done; over. Whatever goodness is coming, I am truly looking forward to this goodness.

As people of this world, we truly need to get a hold of ourselves and focus on our life as well as, ensure this craziness do not happen again. *We cannot afford to let evil people take our life from us by using us as their target practice for Death.*

Black Lands need to get a hold of themselves and clean up the mess they've created on land, and amongst our people; each other.

Right now; as Blacks, we have all to lose, and nothing to gain. We need to start cleaning up our self and the lands; Black Lands we are in.

We can no longer live by the White Man's Ways.

We can no longer comply with their sins, sinful doctrines, sinful way of life, and living.

We need to start living clean lest we are going to be enslaved again.

We can no long discard life for fools' gold come on now. Many Black Lands were colonized, and evil introduced to all in the form of thievery, whoredom, alcohol, diseases, guns, drugs, lies, death, and more.

Figure it out because Blacks were raped of it all, and we are still being raped of it all. Do not be like the Black so-called educated fools that live to kill. Think, and be wise. Figure it out.

It's May 5, 2020 and my dream world is okay.

Dreamt Jennifer Lopez this morning. I can't remember what she was doing. I am not sure if she was singing and dancing, but her face was red. More like a lava colour than red. Did not care for the dream because in the dream I said, she just do anything for money.

The day before that, I dreamt this light engine plane crashed. There were two white gentleman that seemed like they were military sitting, and I was talking to them. The crash appeared in the newspaper and I told them I saw the crash before it happened. I said something else to them. I am not sure if I said I wrote about this.

Anyway, there's going to be more plane crashes. And yes, at the time of editing this book; a Snowbird plane crashed.

In regard to life, it is going to get better. I did dream it was going to get better. But as humans we must know that when you have evil running the globe, evil will create chaos, evil must kill, and we as humans are the guinea pigs for those in power.

This pandemic did not have to be, but it was. So right now, we are in the storm, and after the storm comes a calm until these evil bastards; beings find something else to destroy us with.

Like I tell you, check your environment – the trees because I know it's something that was sprayed in the air. Your environment – trees are your telltale sign therefore, I do not know why humans do not see the environment they live in, and the environment around them.

It is only when humans start seeing their life in life maybe then each one will see the importance of their life.

Right now, *our life hath no merit to those that run the globe.* If our life had merit to them, Earth would not be run like this. Earth would not be dying due to greed; the greed of them that think they can escape the perils of Earth.

It's a fool that think they can escape death.

NO ONE CAN ESCAPE DEATH IF THEIR NAME IS IN THE BOOK OF DEATH. So, no matter where you run, Death will find you. You can run to the Moon, Death will find you because everywhere we as humans go, Life and Death go with us. This many of you will not comprehend because many truly do not know what constitutes life, and what constitutes death.

Right now, *Earth is run by the inept therefore, it's only a matter of time before humans cease to exist literally.*

It's May 6, 2020 4:28am, and I can't go back to sleep. Being warned about Jamaica again. Yesterday, I was telling my daughter that I wanted to go back home. I am fed up of Canada. She put me back on track. See, although I am writing; doing what I was asked to do by God, I am fed up of writing therefore, I truly want to break my order with God.

Yes, I need to stay my ground, but I don't want to anymore. The road at times with God is truly hard, and I can't take any more disappointment. And Yes, I am being selfish. With what's happening globally, I should be thankful, but I am not in some way.

Listen, if I said God has not provided for me during this pandemic, I would be a categorical liar because *God has, and have provided for me and my family.*

I was not on panic mode like millions if not billions.

I had food to eat. Everything I needed I got. Therefore, God is truly maintaining me.

So yes, my daughter is keeping me grounded and, reminding me of issues I will have if I returned to Jamaica.

It's funny, no not funny. Yesterday, I dreamt my great grandmother. She was picking Ackee. Meaning, she was taking the Ackee Fruit out of the pod and throwing it on the ground by the gate leading up to her house, and I was picking the Ackee Fruit with the Black Seed intact off the ground.

I truly do not know what his dream mean. Old death I know is new death and that's about it. Apart from that, I know more death is coming on my mother's side of the family. It's a matter of when.

Now this morning I am being warned about Jamaica. Dreamt my sister's husband's mother. She was telling me people are dying in Jamaica, and I want to go back. I told her Clarendon's death toll has risen 9%.

Trust me, in the dream I kept seeing young men dying; being killed. There was so much death that I am truly tired of seeing the death of people. It is so not healthy spiritually, and physically. So yes, I am seeing more death in Jamaica.

After that and still in Jamaica. I was at a venue; musical venue with stairs. Lady Saw; Marion Hall was singing, and you could see her coming down the stairs singing while girls danced, and gyrated themselves on the stairs. Different female artists were on the venue. I can't remember if it's Heels High she was singing. To the way she was going on I said, I thought she became a Christian. Plus, with how the girls were dancing, I was ashamed; meaning, their dancing did not sit well with me.

After that – seeing the different female deejays singing and or, deejaying, I was in another area and Mr. Vegas, and other male artists were singing – going down the line singing. One touched me microphone that hung down in the air, and I did the same. They were singing this song *and Mexico was apart of the song.* **I don't know what Mexico did, but it was as if they were warning Mexico not to trouble them.**

Continuing on, I was now outside and looking at the stage that would remind me of a Chinese Home to the left of me. Think Chinese traditional home. Corbin Bleu was now in the dream. He climbed up the stage – the part of the stage that looked like a Traditional Chinese Home and the platform came crashing down on him. He was hit so bad that he was crushed. Lady Saw was hurt, this other artist; white that would remind me of Damian Marley's mother, but it wasn't her, and this other female singer. All three were hurt, and they were saying where is Corbin Bleu. They did not see him.

After that happened, I saw my sister, my cousin, and my dead mother. My mother was encased in glass and she was with my cousin, and sister. There was about 6 of my mother encased in glass, glass mirrors. Turning before me and with my mothers, sister, and cousin behind me, there was glass, and parrots were in glasses – mirrors. Someone; but you could not see the person was taking pictures and I said, don't do that. It was like this blockage; someone was using stones to block what they were doing. Taking their picture, you saw the square stone block. Think tile with a creamy pink hue. Then I saw this Black Man in dark clothing behind this mirror. He reached in with one hand and took up a parrot.

Now I can't go back to sleep.

There is so many things happening here that someone is doing some Obeah and or, Voodoo shit that they think is not being seen.

Therefore, whomever is using any form of evil to hurt my family, I am warning you. Truly do not do it. I do not know who you are but, leave my family alone because none is interfering in your life, and nasty life.

So, this morning as I pray, I pray all that is using evil; going to the dead to hurt my family through death, *I pray their evil and evils be truly returned to them.* I see it, and pray to God for whom I call Lovey to protect my family, and let no harm or death befall us in any way by the hand and hands of the wicked; wicked and evil people that do not like us.

Yes, I know there are evil people out there, and it's only going to get worse.

As for Mexico, I truly do not know what is going to happen to that land, and why these male Jamaican artists were singing; warning Mexico.

As for Corbin Bleu, I truly do not know. I think he's of Jamaican descent. He's an American, and he's married to a Canadian I believe.

In regards to China, I truly do not know what structure is going to collapse there.

So, from Canada to the United States of America, to Mexico, to Jamaica, to China, I truly do not know. **Nor do I know if an earthquake is going to ravage these lands with China being heavily hit.**

I do not want to speculate but more death is coming to Jamaica, and my family.

This dream do not really scare me, but it does disturb me. I just have to watch and see.

And yes, I went back to bed and had other dreams.

I dreamt I was moving.

I also dreamt the current President of the United States; Donald Trump. A young Donald Trump that looked as if he was wearing eye make-up, and was drunk.

Trust me, after seeing Donald Trump I woke up out of my sleep gagging as if I was going to vomit. Therefore, wow to evil; the evils of this man because he's a true demon. You will not comprehend but I know. Therefore, when you see the sins of man you can vomit to how wicked; vile they are. Meaning, the amount of sin they have on them and around them.

Politicians are hell bound therefore, you see and know their hell if you are a Chosen of Life; God.

Michelle

It's May 8, 2020, and I am losing track of the days again. Spent time at my dad's and it was a blessing for me. Going back soon. My health is not severe when I am at my dad's. Coming back home my health is beginning to take a toll on me.

Too much negative energy in my home; apartment.

Anyway. My dreams are wow.

Dreamt Tom Cruise, and Ben Stiller. I truly do not want to get into the full details when it comes to this dream because the dream was explicit. With Tom Cruise and Ben Stiller having dinner, and after dinner…you use your mind when it comes to foreplay and sex, with Tom Cruise liking the fact that he was engaging in male to male adult sex, and foreplay with Ben Stiller. In the dream, Tom Cruise seem to be openly gay, he did not shy away from what Ben Stiller did to him.

So yes, I will leave his; Tom Cruise's personal life alone; nor will I decipher this dream. It is not my concern if he Tom Cruise is gay and or, bi-sexual. It's his business, and his business alone. His sexuality truly do not concern me, and never will. Scandal I truly do not like…leave it alone Michelle.

After that, seeing Ben Stiller and Tom Cruise, I was in Florida. I was walking and was openly fired upon by someone I could not see. Wesley Snipes was in the dream. He was in a gray suit. He got shot in the foot; leg and was bleeding. He did not see who shot him, but I saw. In the dream, I was going to do something, but I cannot tell you what. I don't think what I was going to do was nice; legal. Going to Wesley Snipes side I told him I saw the guy that did this. I was trying to show Wesley Snipes the guy, but Wesley could not see him. The guy ghosted himself. I was the only one that could see him; the guy that shot Wesley Snipes. Oh man, how do I describe him. He had a black suit on, black hair in ponytail, with a black gun case in his hand. He was walking towards this bank. So, I do not know if someone is going to open fire on someone in a bank in the United States. He was tall. Okay, the best way for me to describe this guy is; if you pull up the video WIN by Kiprich. The guy that was set up would remind me of the guy, but think white guy with a bigger nose – straight nose.

After that David Caruso was in the dream. Wesley was to go with him but did not. Wesley took the bushes – went through this bushy path.

I ended up in this place; no, I ended up in church with Spanish people especially young Spanish children say around 8-10 years old. This one particular child; boy who was short with short black hair and very handsome had a gun. He was upset at someone. I told him I was going to tell his parents he had a gun, and asked whose child is this, but no one answered. I think I took the gun from him and then we ended up with Wesley Snipes. This child and another one around twelve to fourteen was now in hotel attire. Wesley Snipes had enlisted them to aid him.

After that I do not know what happened. I was now with the short Spanish Child – boy around 8-10 years old. He had a change of clothes on. Meaning, he was no longer in his hotel attire. We were walking and we saw Black Boys and, Mixed Race Boys sitting and eating. Some were heavily tattooed. Some were showing their gang signs, and they knew the young Spanish Child; Boy I was with because they greeted him, and he replied. One tall Black Youth I asked what he wanted to do, and he said; *"he wanted to Rap and if he couldn't Rap, he was going to KILL PEOPLE."*

What he said; the Young Black Youth; lanky Black Youth said disturbed me in the living.

Walking, and leaving the young Spanish Boy behind, I met up with this Young Black Man say; in his late twenties early thirties who was dressed in blue. I think he had blue gloves on as well. I so can't remember if he had red in his hair. I know he was medium built. He said something to me about praying for the boys – **Black Boys.** I said, *"I WOULD NEVER PRAY FOR THEM,"* and waved him off with my hand and continued on my journey until I ended up in Jamaica. The land looked good as if flourishing. You could see the different venders on the street, but the businesses were closed. I was with this Black Lady and I wanted to go to the bathroom. She took me to where I could pee because I really wanted to go. We passed this old and or, dry red outdoor toilet that was broken. We ended up at the second one. The second was broken this girl said. I got a pail to pee in and so did the lady that was with me. Now, I saw the hole; pit that was exposed. I did not go over to the pit toilet. All I did was try to lift my dress of yellow and other colours up to pee right where I was. I was not ashamed to bend down and pee right there. Lifting my dress to pee, I could not get my dress up because it was too tight on my skin.

So, I do not know if Wesley Snipes and David Caruso is/are going to do a movie or, if Ben Stiller and Tom Cruise is/are going to do a movie – but I highly doubt it with Tom Cruise and Ben Stiller. Not a movie of that explicit nature.

Also, I do not know if sink holes are going to open up in Jamaica by an Earthquake, or a Tsunami.

As for the Young Black Youths, I am truly disturbed by what I see when it comes to them. What the hell has gotten into them; our Black Youths Globally?

If you can't Rap, you are going to murder people. *What the hell kind of purpose do you have in life?*

Why would you want to murder people?

What purpose do you serve anyone in the Black Race?

Death is not the answer to Life. Death is the answer to Death. But then again, Gangs are of Death. These young youths Death own. *Some had the MARKINGS OF DEATH on them thus; they had no soul.*

So yes, there is going to be more Black deaths – Black Youths are going to die somewhere in the United States of America. And no, these deaths do not have to be in Florida. With my dream world these deaths can be in the state David Caruso, and Wesley Snipes were born.

Trust me, *I am sickened at the way Black Youths are killing themselves. RAP MUSIC IS THE DEVIL'S MUSIC WE KNOW THIS.* Originally, Rap did not start out this way. But the now Rap Music of today is influenced and owned by the Devil. No good can come out of this genre of music anymore. *And yes, Dancehall that glorifies killing is no better.*

Many in the Dancehall Community have to bow down to Satan. Thus, many have no soul. They sold their soul for money and fame literally. One of the most disgusting dancehall songs for me is *Madable Sick* by Mad Cobra, and Bounty Killer. Thus, *"Satan gave him (Mad Cobra) his credit card."* Thus, Mad Cobra and Bounty Killer hath no soul. Satan literally owns them.

Trust me, if I had power globally, I would ban/bar these two from entering my land; any land of God period. Satan is their god therefore, access denied to all the Lands of Life.

We as Black people have, and has lost our way. We cannot blame anyone for the true demise and or, final demise of the Black Race. We are the ones to glorify death without knowing that when we glorify death, *death must take you in the end.*

Why?

Why?

Why?

What has the Black Race become for us to *KILL FOR A PLACE IN HELL WITH DEATH?*

Are we that stupid that we cannot see that we are dying – taking our self from Life – God literally?

Now let me ask you this; *WHAT THE HELL DID WE LEARN FROM SLAVERY?*

For some absolutely nothing to want to be enslaved again. Yes, I said Slavery is over, but slavery is truly not over for the Black Race. It seems we like the frigging punishment we get.

Wake the Bleep up. The state Blacks are in should have never been. Yet we adopt all the wrongs in life and end up killing our self in the process. *We are not thinking therefore, we are not living.*

When will we wake up and see what we are doing to self and others; other Blacks in our communities globally?

Look at the wrongs of the White Race on a whole. Now tell me, *why is it legal for governments to kill, and illegal for citizens to kill?*

Why are there different sets of laws for the different governments globally, corporations globally, and you the citizen globally?

If one of the laws of Moses states; *"thou shalt not kill,"* why are governments sending our children on the Battlefield of Death to Kill?

Do your government not disobey God, and get you the citizen to disobey God?

So, where is justice here on Earth if we live in systems that encourage us to break all the laws of life?

When the paid assassins of the governments kill, they are deemed heroes, but when you the average citizen kill, you are deemed a monster; murderer; vile, and without a heart. Now tell me, what is the difference in Death; do you both not kill?

So why is one deemed a hero, and the other not?

Do you not both work for Death?
Do you not both kill for Death; a place in hell?
Do you not both void your life with God?

Therefore, man cannot be just if the laws are unjust, and the laws are unjust. Therefore, no one can live in peace, or true peace in unjust societies; the unjust societies of the White Race, and Babylon.

The laws of the White Race and Babylon is truly not right yet, we as Blacks cannot break away from them, and see the evils that are impacting our life individually, and as a whole; community globally.

We pray, we cry, we pray, we cry, we fall down, and we are truly not rising because we continue to live wrong. Accept the wrongs of the different nations. We are the ones to give up right to live in sorrow; pain.

Look at the world around you. If the White Man's Systems are failures; complete failures; why continue to live in them?

If the White Man's Systems encourage you to break the Laws of Life; God, why stay in them?

Why build these evil lands that cause you to sin; die?

The White Man has, and have depleted the resources of Earth due to greed literally; why continue to build them financially?

This race; the White Race is destroying this planet including you. Nothing good can come out of evil yet, billions live by evil; kill each and every day. So now tell me, *if you disrespect self and others, how can you, or will you respect God; all life?*

If someone, or something is causing you pain; slowly move away, and build yourself good and true come on now. Do not stay in abuse come on now.

As Blacks, we are the ones that refuse to break away from the lies of the different nations.

We are the ones that like the false education we receive.

<u>A NATION BUILT ON LIES CAN NEVER SUCCEED. THAT NATION WILL FAIL,</u> and Blacks are failing. We've accepted the false teachings of our enemies, rebuilt our land and life with these false systems now look at the different Black Lands Globally.

Failure beget failure.

The White Man's System is failure period.

No one can live in failure and think they can succeed; you will never succeed. You will forever be in debt period.

Anyone that emulate, and live for failure; meaning, live by the White Way; the White Man's Way <u>will forever be in debt.</u> No, don't go there. Like I said in other books. <u>If your beginning is dirty, your end will be dirty also.</u> So, false beginnings produce false endings. You can never be right.

So, if you believe the lies of the bible then; God cannot be with you because, God is clean not dirty.

Trust me. When you live in the White Man's way, you are not rich. but <u>"living in debt."</u>

***"I have money, my country has money, we/my country have resources that we sell to the different nations"** many of you are saying. But with all that money look at your land. Look at the living situations of some in your land. Now take a look at the environment, the loss of trees, the air pollution, lack of clean drinking water. Now tell me, are you rich or are you in debt?*

With all you do, your riches that you have, have you not taxed you; put your country in debt environmentally, physically, health wise, spiritually, sin wise, and more?

Now let me ask you this; <u>what did it cost you, and future generations right now?</u>

What good and true legacy are you, and your land leaving behind for future generations?

Will your future generations not take on your debt?

What about their debt; the debt of your future generations that they will incur?

So how rich are you when God will not bless your land; refuse to bless your land?

Did God not walk away from many lands globally?

So, how far are you going to get in life when the door(s) of God is truly closed to you and your land including, people?

God walked away from Jamaica I know this for a fact; so, what say you?

Going back to what the Young Black Youth said. It's unbelievable how we as Black People give up our life for a place in hell. I know for a fact that Hell is real. <u>I see the hell of some people, and can tell them their hell before they die.</u>

But dear God to want to kill people. Yes, I am an advocate for Death to go with their wicked and evil own yes, but wow when it comes to the younger generation of Black Youths. Many truly have no place in life period.

Listen, I talk to my children. Despite my pain with them; I do talk to them, and some of the things they are telling me I have to wonder why some men and women have children because they are so bleeping worthless it's not funny.

But you know what, let me leave things alone. <u>It's us as Blacks that do not want true life.</u> For this young man to say what he said in my dream; <u>we as Blacks have and has lost it all. We are frigging valueless thus, the different nations can use us as their scapegoats including our demented own.</u>

2020 has been a year of Death and Dismay for many. For me, I would like to travel out, but I need to wait until 2021.

You know, the more I live is the more I see just how demented; wicked and evil some in society are globally, and I truly would like to move away from society.

<u>Right now, we are in an era of Chemical Warfare and or, Biological Warfare with one Race; the White Race thinking they have control over it all. If they can't bully you, they are going to destroy you; kill you because they feel they are the dominant race, and they can get away with the evils that they do.</u>

No, I am tired of this race literally with the evils they are doing here on Earth to destroy everything including Earth herself.

So many has and have died of Covid-19, but like my niece said to me. With the blood tests/the tests they are taking, **<u>what would stop them; these evil bastards from saying it's</u>**

Covid-19 to hike the number of deaths knowing full well not all these deaths are from Covid-19.

So, God is never wrong, and can never be wrong when it comes to the White Race of Murderers that dominate this Earth.

Their life is an act. Therefore, they act out the evils they are going to do to you in their movies.

Look at the movie <u>**CONTAGION**</u> because the movie did tell you the next wave of horror by Corporate America, and their Government. *The movie is spot on. Thus, Movies are codes for those high up.* Their way; evil way of telling their own; those above them what they are going to do globally to the different nations to keep their place in hell with Death thus, *ensuring their loyalty to Death.* As well as, ensuring they still have success; dirty money they use to pay their people that aid them in murdering others globally.

The Bible of Man – the White Race is a book of codes; lies that they the White Race was going to use to get humans globally to succumb to their way of lies hence, the religions they give you to deceive nations. Thus, taking God from billions literally. But then **Death is the fault of humans literally.**

You do not kill to live, you live to live. **No human can claim Earth as their own because, Earth belongs to none.** Earth belong to her; Earth. Each human has and have a life expectancy due to sin, and the sins of others. So, when any think they can bypass death, they had better think again.

ALL IN THE WHITE RACE HAVE TO; MUST ANSWER FOR THEIR SINS.

NONE CAN OR WILL ESCAPE THEIR JUDGEMENT. Just as those Blacks who have given up their life must face their judgement, *the White Race MUST FACE THEIR JUDGEMENT TOO.*

Every individual that has, and have sinned is held accountable for their sins.
Each sin is recorded, and each good you do is recorded.

Listen, *Earth is the Realm of choice as well.* Therefore, the choice to live, and the choice to die that we all make.

Remember White People, **you cannot run from your lies.** Not one of you can. *Remember your so - called holy bible. King James Bible, and other Bibles. That Book; your* *so-called holy book of garbage is a testament of your lies, and how far you would go with your lies.*

You lied on God period. You failed; did not tell nations your God is Death. Thus, all the lies you tell on life literally, and period you must pay for.

Now let me ask you this; **DO YOU TRULY BELIEVE THAT DEATH WILL, AND WOULD LET YOUR RACE GO FREE?**

DO YOU TRULY BELIEVE THAT DEATH WILL FORGIVE YOU FOR YOUR LIES TOLD ABOUT AND AGAINST GOD; LIFE?

Death will never pardon any of you because Death cannot pardon anyone.

So no, God for whom I call Lovey from time to time truly have nothing to worry about when it comes to Death consuming your race; the White Race for the lies you have told on God; all Life period.

Death has virtually all of you locked in hell. The final toll has begun. Your past is of death, your present is of death, and your future including tomorrow is of death. So, tell me; how clean are the lots of you when God knows you not?

My job is done. It is up to God now, and the next Chosen to advocate for life; the life of their people.

You the White Race had a chance. Instead of choosing life for your race, you chose Death. Hence <u>**CAIN DID KILL ABEL.** *Yes, carried the **CURSE OF DEATH,***</u> and passed it on through his bloodline literally.

Your race failed period. So, because your race failed, you've caused the Black Race to fail. Now you are targeting the Chinese Race.

Life must move on to the next Chosen Race, and that's the Chinese Race. I know this.

God cannot give power unto people who defy God, lie on God, do all to kill Life, and more.

Lies cannot save anyone. Lies can only destroy and kill you, and this is exactly what you the White Race has and have done. Killed others including yourself.

NATURAL MYSTIC – Robert Nesta Marley aka, Bob Marley. He did tell you more death was to come but none listened to him. He knew of the mystics thus, Blacks have and has lost their mystical powers literally. *And yes, you can go back in the past. I do via my dream world.*

TIME WILL TELL – Robert Nesta Marley aka, Bob Marley. Bob Marley specifically told you God would not give his power to a Baldhead. Anyone evil for that matter. So yes, the White Race is literally living in hell because your time is up; will tell.

Thus, I dedicate *TIME WILL TELL* by Robert Nesta Marley aka, Bob Marley to every White Person that fall under the White Banner of Death.

Michelle

It's May 11, 2020. It snowed.

No, let me leave the environment.

Dreamt Dennis Rodman. He had a disease; AIDS, and he passed it on to me and ran away.

<u>Therefore, BLACK FEMALES BE ON YOUR GUARD WHEN IT COMES TO THE MEN YOU ARE LAYING WITH, GOING TO LAY WITH AND OR, HAVING SEXUALY INTERCOURSE, OR INTIMATE RELATIONS WITH.</u>

<u>SOMEONE HAS AN INCURABLE STI, AND THEY ARE GOING TO SPREAD IT IN THE BLACK COMMUNITY.</u> <u>**You are being warned.**</u>

Further, keep vigilant when it comes to any new vaccines they are going to unload on Blacks globally.

You do not want to be chipped by them – our enemies globally.

Therefore, you know some of our Black Own truly do not care about your health and safety. Their mind; thought is sick therefore, our own do kill us; have no good will, or true good will for their Black Own.

And, because I see Dennis Rodman; does not mean it's him to be spreading a disease. Black People in my dream can represent the land and or, state things are going to spread and or, happen in.

Michelle

It's May 13, 2020 5:17 am, and I can't go back to sleep. I so don't know but I know. It's still cold here in Canada. Still getting spirts of snow here and there, and this is supposed to be Spring.

So not going to worry about the climate, and the environmental changes that is happening here on Earth. Humans have already doomed Earth, and the environment of Earth due to greed.

Yesterday, was a day for me in the sense that I was seeing faces; Black Female Faces before me. I would say these females were in their late twenties, early thirties. I can remember one particular one; Black Female lying on her back. She had a bald head and was beautiful. Then I saw this other Black Female. **She was hanging from a noose, and she was spinning around.** I could not get rid of that sight; seeing this Black Female with a noose around her neck spinning. Oh man; I so don't want to describe her. I would say around 150 to 160 pounds give or take a couple of pounds. Dark complexion. Everyone of the females were dark skinned. This particular Black Female who had the noose around her neck had nappy hair that was not too short. I would say her hair length was about 4 to 6 inches but not greater.

I can't fully remember her attire. I know blue and white were in her attire; skirt of blue; very light blue.

I do not know why she was hanging outside of what would look like an olden day store front that reminded you of a house; home. So yes, more Black Females are going to die, and hang themselves, or be hanged.

These waking state visions were so vivid that if I could draw; sketch the faces of these Black Females I would for you to see the beauty of them, and the ugliness of some. Beauty turning into ugliness.

I am so not going to worry about my waking state visions of faces – Black Female Faces because these visions I cannot fully pinpoint so I do not focus on them, or put any merit to them in that way apart from death – those who are going to die shortly somewhere in the world.

As for my dreams. I can't fully remember if I dreamt my mother again. Yes, for some; frequent dreams of a loved one who have passed away in the flesh can, and do signify/mean birth. For me, and in my family it's both; death, and birth.

This particular dream wow. I was somewhere. I cannot tell you where other than hell in some way. I have to say hell because the dream is disturbing, and disgusting.

Dear God for you White People because, **none of you know your hell literally.** In the dream, *this man; brown skinned Man who was filthy – so disgusting you saw the dirty; muddy dirt; filth of him on him.* He was so disgusting that thinking of him, and writing this portion of the dream make me sick to how disgusting this man looked. **He was on my right, and this White Man was shackled – tie up with his hand up on my left.** He too was dirty, and this White Girl with black hair was tied up also, and she was dirty as well. *They were bound, and the filthy man was speaking – judging them.* I did not know why he was judging them, **nor did I know why he bound them like slaves.** He continued to talk, and I said something to him in protest of bounding these people. He did not say anything to me but continued to judge these people. Oh man, **_I cannot fully remember if Canada was judged, and found guilty also._** With him not saying anything to me, this short Black Man – midget said something, and went to the filthy brown skinned man that was judging the White Man and Woman. He said something to the filthy brown skinned man and this door – think fenced zinc door that you would see when someone closeup their shop. Think fenced zinc door that some in Los Angeles use to lock up and or, down their business. This was the fenced zinc door that came down to close off the White Man, and White Woman individually.

After that, *I was with the Woman of Zion.* *She agreed with what the filthy brown skinned man did to the White Man, and White Woman.* I did not agree with her, and was upset at her; the Woman of Zion in the dream.

So yes, for me; *this dream signals the judgement, and hell of White People.* They have been judged, and Canada has been judged also. So, I truly do not know what is going to happen to Canada judgement wise, nor do I know what is going to happen to the White Race Globally.

All I know is, *there is no heaven for White People with God.* **They've been found guilty, and now they must face their hell.** *I could not save them;* thus, the filthy man closed the door on them; this White Man, and White Woman individually literally.

So yes, the White Race will be enslaved in hell literally. *You do not kill to live, you live to live.*

You do not lie on God and think you will not face your judgement. Religion, and religious lies.

You do not create chaos, and death here on Earth and think you won't/will not face your judgement. Politics, and Political Wars that pit humans against humans, humans against God, God against humans, animals, our environment, our God Given Life, and more.

No one can kill to live. They can only kill to die, and this is what's happened to you in the White Race. Yes, many in the Black Race are going to die because they've given up life for Death. Trust me, I will not cry for any in the White Race because their evils has, and have gone too far.

When you choose Death over life this is what you get; Death. So, like I said in other books. *IF YOUR BEGINNING IS DIRTY, YOUR END MUST BE DIRTY ALSO.* Yes, the White Man's beginning is dirty, thus their end is also dirty. It is a dirty; truly filthy brown skinned man that is so disgusting that judged them; the White Race as well as; CLOSED THE DOOR ON THEM; THE WHITE RACE AND RIGHTFULLY SO.

So yes, the trumpet has sounded, and there is no going/turning back for the White Race and Canada. For Canada, **you do not say you are a peace keeping country and side with Death against life.** You will be judged, and Canada was judged. When you say you are of Peace and go against Life; God is truly against you because you are disrespecting God; all life. You are also lying to God. You do not turn your back on God if you are of God no matter your hurt and pain. Yes, at times I want to leave God, but I have to stay my ground.

Life is worth it and it's us as humans that give up life as well as, **let others take life from us.** As humans we need to think and put God first. Meaning, let God be your mainstay because our actions; sins do judge us, and many are judged physically and spiritually literally. Many have not life therefore they cannot live; see God.

So yes, it's a matter of time before Physical Time reaches that time in time (Spiritual Time), and all come tumbling down for everyone in the White Race including Canada.

Listen, *it's a fool that say;* *"GOD IS THE ONE TO JUDGE US." God cannot judge anyone and will never ever judge anyone.* **Our sins; evils and or, bad and or, wrong actions judge us.**

God did not create our hell for us. We as individuals created our own hell with the Sin, and Sins we do each and every day. Some, our parents created our hell for us, and so on.

Yes, many say our children are a blessing, and our children can save us. True, **but how many of our children are born clean?**

Many parents do take the saving grace of their children from them. So, for those who are banking on their children saving them, **truly better think and remember how they had their children.**

Some children are born from adulterous relationships.

Yes, adultery is forgiven, but when it comes to having children out of adulterous unions, I truly do not know if this is forgiven. When I do find out, I will let you know. And although adultery is forgiven. *When you know what constitutes adultery, and continually go into adulterous relationships then adultery is not forgiven.* You know what adultery is so stay out of adulterous relationships – unions.

Okay, many of you do not know of my other books on Lulu.com. This is a new outlet for me, and I am hoping all goes well for me depending on if Lulu.com fix their issues in time for me to upload this book on another outlet.

But, you have some women that register their children wrong. Meaning, person X is the father of that child, but the mother gave person W the child, and registered the child in person W's name knowing full well that person X is the father. Because she; the mother has and have knowingly registered her child and or, that child wrong. Her child; son, or daughter cannot have life, nor can that child save her. She the mother took her child's right to life from him or her. This is how I know it, and this is how I am relating it back to you.

So, when the time of saving comes, that child cannot be saved, nor will the mother. She took life from herself and that child. She sent that child to hell because life; the Life of God have to/must pass over and or, pass that child by. God know not that child because the mother gave that child to death. She registered her child wrong therefore, God cannot have anything to do with him or her; that child.

There's a lot of things that we as humans do that take Life; the Life of God from us. Therefore, I tell you; *"THE WHITE MAN'S GOD IS NOT THE BLACKMAN'S GOD."*

THE TRUE GOD OF LIFE CANNOT TAKE LIFE FROM ANYONE NOR DOES GOD TAKE LIFE FROM ANYONE. DEATH IS THE ONE TO TAKE THE FLESH, AND SPIRIT NOT GOD.

So, know the difference between Life and Death. There is Life after the flesh is gone and there is also Death. So, know where you stand in Life. Do not wait until you die to know where you belong.

So, when you listen to false teachings; lies; the lies of the White Race, and live by the lies of the White Race then you forfeit life. Billions have forfeited life thus God cannot, and will never ever worry about billions. God can only worry about and or, save the good and true of Earth, and the Spiritual Realm.

Religion is truly not of God therefore the beginning of Man is dirty. Further, *because the beginning of Man is dirty, Man must end dirty and you see this from my dream.* The judgement has and have begun, it is only a matter of time before this judgement reaches Earth.

Absolutely no one can blame God for the demise of humans. Humans have to blame humans *because billions DID ACCEPT LIES OVER THE TRUTH.*

Billions globally bow down to Death.
Billions live for Death.
Billions pay homage to Death.
Billions pay Death to kill them. See your tides and offerings.

Billions side with their political leaders and go on the Battlefield of Death to kill thus forfeiting their life.

Billions use religion as a pass without knowing; religion is dirty, of Death therefore, forfeiting their life.

So, in all humans do. *Humans has and have done nothing to preserve themselves; their life with God.* God was never the enemy, and will never ever be the enemy. Humans are the enemies of God because humans lie on God, disrespect God, take life from self and others including, the land we live in, and the planet we call home.

Instead of going to God with our concerns, we turn to man for help.
Instead of talking to God about our problems, we confess them to man.

So, because we as humans put Man over God, God cannot help us; well billions.

The problems of Earth is/are truly not due to God, but due to us as humans.

You cannot side with Death and think God is going to save you. God will not save you. God will, and do step aside, and let Death have their way with you literally.

SO, THE JUDGEMENT OF THE WHITE RACE IS DUE TO THE WHITE RACE. THEY CANNOT, AND WILL NEVER EVER SEE THEIR EVILS OF THE PAST UNTIL NOW, AND CHANGE THEIR DIRTY LINEN OF SELF. All they do to deceive nations they think is right. They are doing the right thing.

Know for a fact. <u>Their life; the Life of the White Race is an act</u> therefore, their history, life, well being, state of disarray, dysfunction, lies, murder, religious genocide, chemical and germ warfare, wars, religious wars, greed, and so much more <u>is played out in the movies.</u> All the evils that they do is recorded in history. From the past until now. So no, <u>NO ONE BLACK CAN SAVE THIS RACE ANYMORE. THEY THE WHITE RACE ARE CUT OFF FROM LIFE; GOD AND RIGHTFULLY SO.</u>

It's death at all cost for this race.

If they; the White Race cannot have dominion over all they were going to destroy it all, and this is what they are doing.

They; the White Race must lie.
They; the White Race must deceive.
They; the White Race must create war, and strife; kill.

They; the White Race are true killing machines therefore, virtually all of them are hell bound literally without doubt. Judgment has started for them spiritually. <u>*Therefore Lovey, you must manifest; let the destruction of the White Race happen here on Earth as well.*</u> *You cannot show me the spiritual destruction; condemnation, and hell of Whites in the spiritual realm without letting this destruction; condemnation and judgement happen here on Earth. Every nation and or, individual here on Earth that is hell bound you must let them know their hell. Let them know they are truly cut off from all life period. Earth has been judged therefore, humans must be judged here on Earth, and all who are hell bound hell, their hell must receive them literally.*

Their; the White Race's judgement is coming. Like I said, it's a matter of time when Physical Time reaches that point in time; Spiritual Time then all will come tumbling down for the White Race because; <u>*"THEY CANNOT BE SAVED."*</u>

So, as Jamaica is deemed unclean by God, and I've deemed the United States of America unclean particularly LA (Los Angeles) all must come crashing down for these lands. Now Canada is being judged. So yes, woe be unto man; humans literally. We keep ignoring life and think that all is going to be okay in the end. <u>*As Blacks we continually fail Life; God.*</u> Every land of Death must go with Death Lovey. These lands must be judged as well including the people of the land.

Their; the White Race's wickedness throughout history is a testament of how far this race will go to manipulate, destroy, and kill.

As for me Lovey, I am fed up of Blacks Globally. *I've told you in other books to have ambition for yourself.* Blacks throughout the centuries have and has proven to you that they do not want you in their life so leave them; those Blacks that don't want you alone. Slam your door in their face literally. Turn the tides on them; those Blacks that do not want or need you. *Give them; those Blacks that do not want or need you the F YOU SIGN, turn up your loudspeakers and blast the song TOO LATE for them to hear.* Mek dem more dan weep now. Yes, I know it's something I would do, but you have to let ungrateful people that use the colour of their skin as a bly.

Blacks Globally have become the muse for the different races therefore, WE HAVE FALLEN FROM GRACE; YOUR GRACE LOVEY. So, F Blacks literally. Blacks has and have become the FALLEN ANGELS of man's so-called holy bible literally.

Look at the way we treat each other.
Kill each other.
Cut down each other.

Have become demons that are so tattooed that none know that tattoos are of the devil; your confirmation; mark to Death that you belong to Death literally. Cain of man's so-called holy bible.

This is the final straw for me when it comes to Blacks Lovey. My dream with what the Black Youth said about if he can't Rap, he was going to murder people. Then me talking to this Black Lady about what is happening – Covid-19, and who the true cause of it is, and she looked at me as if I am crazy. She was so complacent with the lies the government and media tell that it's beyond me why you Lovey would want to save Nations of Fools.

Now tell me, what can you as God gain from people who constantly fail you in life?

So no, F Blacks because they truly do not want the truth, nor do they want to know the truth. So yes, it's time to Passover these complacent Sell Out Blacks that feed Death with their life; ignorance.

Like I told you Lovey earlier in my journey with you. I would never ever March for anyone Black or anyone for that matter. I am not a fool to fight for fools that sell you out behind your back.

No Lovey, you are no exception to the rule. How many Blacks has and have sold you out globally from the beginning of time until now? Procreation

Didn't Blacks side with evil against you? Earth, procreation, religion, generational lies, tribal lies, and curses that are handed down from generation to generation.

And you Lovey and excuse me this morning, <u>but you are a true fool to hold on to people that continually sell you out for fools gold; the devil.</u>

See for yourself. See how many Blacks bow down to Death, and praise Death. Africa; the Continent of Africa is a testament of how Blacks has and have walked away from you and HAVE FALLEN FROM GRACE therefore, people can use Black Africans as puppets – their true guinea pigs. See the manmade diseases like AIDS, Ebola, Syphilis, that was brought into Africa to wipe them off the planet. See the major corporations of the globe that own African lands and resources.

<u>*Jamaica is a testament of how vile and nasty some Blacks have become to the point where you Lovey and God has and have deemed Jamaica unclean.*</u> So no, it's time for you Lovey to fully walk away from Blacks. We did deceive self, and we did walk away from life. Trust me, I have no regrets, nor will I get mad at you for walking away from Blacks Globally. You cannot continue to give your life and all to people that truly do not want life. People that has and have given you the F you sign literally.

Let Blacks go. It's time for you Lovey to move on. Look at it. Black Lands Globally are being destroyed and it is us as Blacks that are aiding Death to destroy us.

Lovey I am going to send you somewhere. It's a video. *SEVANA, JAZ ELISE, LILA IKE, AND NAOMI COWEN ROCK & GROOVE RIDDIM FREESTYLE/1XTRA JAMAICA 2020.* <u>*Truly listen to Sevana and what she said about how we are falling, and how we let evil use us.*</u> She is more than infinitely correct. Blacks are the used and abused because we let evil use us, and we ignore all the signs of Life. Therefore, you as God cannot continue to pump life into people that truly do not want or need you in their life. <u>*So yes, let it be done for me by you truly walking away from Blacks; those Blacks that truly do not need or want life with you.*</u> Give the Chinese Zion. But in doing so; giving the Chinese Zion, let the successor in China and or, from the Mongolian and or, Chinese Race look at life from then to now, and plea for good and true life. <u>*Let true goodness be the goal and stay of the next successor not death.*</u> Let the Chinese learn from the mistakes of Babylon, the White and Black Race, and not make the same mistakes as them. Truth must reign supreme good and true here on Earth Lovey come on now. This is the final road for some here on Earth so let it all come crashing down for evil everywhere. Evil cannot recover, and must never recover Lovey come on now.

Yes, I am done now. And yes, I would pay to go to concert just to see these girls; Sevana, Jaz Elise, Lila Ike, and Naomi Cowan perform like this. They are truly talented. Hence, they should collaborate musically all of them like this.

<u>*DON'T BLAME LIFE*</u> *by the reggae artist Bugle.*

As Blacks we cannot *BLAME LIFE FOR OUR DESTRUCTION.* We were the ones to refuse God and no matter how God has tried with us, we did not listen; we kept walking on the wrong path. We did give our wealth and self to our enemies therefore, we were used and abused.

Salvation do not come through religion, false hope, lies, or anything negative. Salvation comes through truth. You knowing the truth, and doing truthful things.

So many have and has tried over the centuries to save us and we keep refusing saving. Therefore, I cannot petition God; Lovey for people that have no worth, net worth, or value in life. Those who are of life must be saved but all others can literally kick rocks because you cannot be saved.

No more must die Lovey trying to save people who truly do not want or need to be saved. If we as Blacks wanted Life; You Lovey, we would not have given up life. We would build life truthfully with you and self.

Life Matters, but to us as Blacks; *BLACK LIFE TRULY DO NOT MATTER.* Therefore, Blacks did abandon Life for Death.

Michelle

<u>*SO MUCH THINGS TO SAY*</u> **by the great Robert Nesta Marley aka, Bob Marley.**

Truly listen to the lyrics of this song.

<u>*Know:*</u>

Absolutely no one can be justified in unjust societies.
Absolutely no one can be justified by the unfair law and laws of men.
Truth will always be the mainstay of life.
Without truth you cannot have life.
Without truth you are dead; living as the dead literally.

Know that when you are walking right and or, trying to walk right in life, you will have obstacles <u>**because the job of evil is to ensure that you fail.**</u> *It matters not if that evil is your spouse, children, mother, father, friends you call family, aunts, cousins, sisters, brothers, and more.* <u>**Evil's job is to destroy and kill.**</u> *When you are walking right; evil set you up, use you, will abuse you. This is the job of evil. Those that/who follow evil, and do for evil have no where to go apart from hell; their hell. Therefore, it is truly up to you to cling solid to Life; God.*

Listen, all some men do is talk, and talk a lot of shit that has and have killed many globally.

The wars of men is/are truly not justified.
The religions of men is/are truly not justified.
<u>**Anything that take you from life is truly not justified.**</u>

Therefore, Death is truly not justified, but Death have to be justified due to our sins literally.

In life you have to know where you stand. **<u>Evil is not just physical but spiritual also;</u>** *with Spiritual Death being the harshest, and deadliest of deaths.* <u>**Yes, you can say life is numbered here on Earth, but for evil; those who have more sins than good, their life in their hell is numberless.**</u>

Further, know that some in the Black Community will set you up. Side with Death to kill you if you go against the beliefs of men. Listen to what Bob Marley said about Jesus Christ, Paul Bogle, and Marcus Mosiah Garvey. Their own Black People set them up <u>**with the exception of Jesus Christ.**</u> *None of you know the truth of Christ – Jesus Christ.*

Listen, Paul Bogle tried to help Jamaicans and Jamaicans killed him.

Marcus Mosiah Garvey tried to help Black Americans, and they Black Americans set him up. Blacks did not want to go back to Africa. Did not want goodness and truth for self.

<u>**TRUE BLACKS ARE TO GO BACK TO AFRICA.**</u> *God did make a way for True Blacks to go back home, and some in the Black Community destroyed that road; the road that Marcus Mosiah*

Garvey was ordained to give them. Therefore, many Blacks say they are with you, but are truly not with you. They will forever be loyal to Death. The lies of the devil suit them just fine. This is good for them but when the fire hits…let me forget it because, <u>I KNOW FOR A FACT THAT MANY BLACKS ARE IN HELL, AND MANY MORE ARE HELL BOUND LITERALLY WITHOUT DOUBT.</u>

Therefore, I tell you in other books. <u>"HELL IS FULL OF BLACK PEOPLE, AND RECRUITING MORE."</u>

Lands are being judged therefore, woe be unto the Global Population of humans literally.

So yes, you have bitches in the Black Race that do to kill you as well. <u>Thus, in all I do, I plea to God for whom I call Lovey from time to time to save not one Black Sell Out Globally but, slam the door real hard in their faces literally. The True Black Race truly do not need them; the Black Sell Outs of the Globe. They are truly not apart of the True Black Race, but are true demons that look, and appear Black but are the devil's spawns; minions that the Devil use as their bitch thus, Black Death literally.</u>

So, don't think that you do not have evil Blacks Globally. I told you about Black Politicians in other books and this book. I've yet to touch on Black Religious Leaders that defy God and sell the devil's agenda to bring their own Black People to hell with them.

<u>We are Black, and we are to know better and uphold the Truth of Life.</u> The White Man is not Black therefore, they cannot tell you about Life; True Black Life, and how you/Blacks came into being; were created. Our origin is not the White Man's origin therefore, we cannot let them teach us about us; Life. They truly do not know or know you.

So no, not all Blacks are Black. Some Blacks are White; fall under the White Banner of Death literally.

Thus, <u>THE LAWS OF MEN CANNOT BE JUSTIFIED BECAUSE THEY; THE LAWS OF MEN ARE TRULY UNJUST.</u> If you are of life, continue on your journey of life. Put all your trust in God, and ensure you have a SAVINGS ACCOUNT WITH GOD. Bank your goodness in God thus your savings account. Ensure you have and or, get interest with God. Meaning, tell God if there is any interest on your goodness to put that interest towards saving a true, and truthful person that you truly love. For example, my mother is the best mother there is. And although she is not with me in the flesh, she is truly apart of my saved. So, my Savings with God goes towards my saved like my mother, myself, God, and the true and good seeds God has, and have given me.

In order for your saved to be saved, you have to let God know whilst you are still alive here on Earth. Once your flesh dies, your goodness stop collecting here on Earth, and I could be wrong, but I truly don't think so. Once your flesh dies; expire, your life here on Earth expires.

So, if you have $1.00 to give to someone; the homeless and or, a friend, do not wait until you die to give it; your goodness through a will. Give your goodness to those that you need to give to little by little while you are alive so that you get that goodness, and the interest of God on that goodness. Get your blessing here on Earth now. And I hope I've explained it correctly.

Yes, you can still have a will to secure your loved ones financially once your spirit leaves the flesh.

As long as <u>YOUR WILL IS GOOD AND TRUE, GOD CANNOT REFUSE YOUR GOOD AND TRUE WILL IF YOU ARE A GOOD PERSON.</u>

The will of those who belong to Death is truly not looked upon by God. Nothing evil do is good, it is evil period.

<u>RIDE NATTY RIDE</u> by the great Robert Nesta Marley aka, Bob Marley.

God will not be head cornerstone for any Black Sell Out. I refuse to let this happen; let God be HEAD CORNERSTONE FOR ANY SELL OUT BLACKS ANYWHERE if I can help it. <u>Thus, my dream of refusing to pray for Black Youths.</u> Youths that have no worth; value in life, and to self. We are destroying our own and no matter how God send people to teach us, we refuse the good counsel of these people. The lies the devil tell suits many in the Black Race just fine because, they are getting what they want here on Earth. But, what happen when the Spirit leave the Flesh?

What about your children; the ones you have, and will have later?

Once you've sold your soul; give up life for Death. All your off springs and future generations belong to Death, they do not fall under the Banner of Life therefore, God cannot and will not save them. Life is truly not with them but Death.

So yes, as Blacks refuse Life; God, I truly hope God continue to refuse these Blacks that refuse life from generation unto generation continually without end. As a matter of fact; all who refuse Life; Good and True Life, I truly hope God continue to refuse these people from generation unto generation continually without end.

Death is your choice so let Death maintain and sustain you period.

Michelle
May 2020

Listen, humans are feeling it right now. We are being killed; there are no and ifs or buts about this. Mass Death must occur for some.

Death is the purpose for many; billions in the world. This is the choice of many; billions, and these billions are entitled to their choice. Therefore, God know them not.

Many are suffering in the Systems of Men globally, but this is their choice as well. We as humans are the ones to procreate illegally. I say illegally because not one of us asked God for righteous, clean, truthful, honest, wise, humble, truly peaceful children, and more. I too am guilty of this. I asked God for children yes, and the name I wanted to name my children but, I did not tell God what characteristics; virtues I wanted and needed in my children. It is later on in my life that I realized; learnt about the Askings of God. Meaning, what I should ask God for. Yes, there are certain things God cannot give you and will never give you because, it is not in God to do so.

Listen, I've been praying to God for a mate for over a decade now, and I still can't receive one. This is because the virtues I need in a partner God cannot find in any human. Yes, I am picky, and this is me. I've learnt the hard way just how deceptive men and women can be therefore, I truly do not need any form of evil around me anymore.

And, not because I have children do not mean that I do not go through pain. I do. I am still going through pain with my adult children. Some do things that are my downfall. It is easier for them to listen to evil, and do evil things rather than listen to good and true counsel therefore, I did not fail as a mother, my children; some are the ones to fail me. And yes, at times I think of myself as a failure when it comes to my children.

In many societies; household especially Black Household, it's mother alone. There are no fathers there to help raise the children, and guide them in life. Therefore, many of our youths fall in the cracks; take up gun, are in gangs, do a lot of evil things. Men; some men truly do not realize that you need to be there for your child. You have to instill good values in your children so they can grow upright to God. And yes, I know some children truly do not want to listen to good and true counsel. I have some. <u>Some listen, but truly do not hear.</u>

Listen, God cannot bless our children if they are not a blessing to God.
God cannot bless me if I am not a blessing to God.
God cannot bless you if you are not a blessing to God.

Yes, the pain is great but like I said earlier; failure begets failure and, humans are failing.

We fail to see life.
Fail to live right.
Fail to accept truth.
Fail to see our flaws; faults.

Fail to see God; the True and Living God.
We fail our children
Fail our society.
Fail our upbringing.
Fail the environment; Earth.

We are failures all around because failure is what we were given to live by, and stand by. Yes, you can dispute this. This is your right. All I write in these books you can dispute. It is your right. God did not give humans anything unclean. We as humans accepted the unclean things we were given by others including, our parents.

If you know something is not right, why do it?

Go to God and ask for clarity; the truth.

You cannot say God will do this, this, and this. God do not have to do anything for any human because humans truly did not choose Life; God for self and family including, future generations. I told you in other books; <u>DEATH IS A GOD.</u>

Death is the God for some therefore, billions kill. Must, and have to kill to maintain their place in hell. So, know you.

Life can be easy for everyone but, for those who control Earth's resources, <u>Life cannot be easy for some.</u> Therefore, unclean societies, unjust law and laws were implemented to keep you down – make you fail in life. <u>Unclean laws only benefit the unclean.</u> These laws do not benefit those who are trying to be good; live right in Life with God. Therefore, the good and true will feel pain and hurt. We will, and do say God has failed us, but God cannot go into unclean places. Therefore, God cannot fail us. As the good and true of life, <u>we need to set up good and true systems for self so that we can grow positive, and live.</u>

<u>We need to support our good and true own only.</u> We can no longer support evil, evil politicians, evil family members, evil friends, the evil clergies; pastors, deacons, priestesses, priests, elders, evil corporations, the Armies of Death globally, and more.

Good must separate from Evil. Therefore, it is unwise to integrate yourself amongst and or, with evil.

<u>As God is separated from all evil, the Children and People of Life; God must separate self from all evil.</u>

It's May 22, 2020 and the crisis is slowing down for me. But is it all over?

No.

Just this week I dreamt God was holding my hand. In the living I told God, I truly do not feel special, <u>and I don't feel special.</u> Maybe it's because I need God to hold my hand each and every day; talk to me. And no, I did not feel the power of God; strength of God therefore, I am left disappointed in that way.

Listen, I am extremely picky when it comes to God, and God knows this. I have to feel your energy; strength. It's just me.

Am I dreaming about China again?

Yes

Trust me when I tell you this. <u>I am being barred big time from seeing into the happenings of China.</u> I do not know why I am being barred because usually I see things in different lands but this land; China, <u>wow to me being locked out of seeing what the Chinese are doing.</u>

I will not question things when it comes to me not seeing into China spiritually and or, dream wise but wow though.

<u>There is something happening in China that someone in the Spiritual Realm truly do not want me to see therefore, they are doing all for me not to see. Trust me, the barring of me is strong.</u>

I do not know who is going to initiate War, but War is inevitable.

I do not know if America is going to start...no, you know what, let me leave this alone because I did dream War for which I put; put what I saw dream wise in another book.

Right now, I have to leave things in God's hands. Many humans globally are sick mentally both physically and spiritually. All that is happening here on Earth is done by diseased people that truly have no merit in life. Well they don't have life due to the ills; vile things they do here on Earth, and in the Spiritual Realm.

Yes, the trees are budding but some look more than half dead to me. So, only God knows when it comes to our environment. And I am hoping that God listen to me and....no, there is more to come therefore, we as humans have to blame self for electing demented, and vile; truly ugly and gross demonic humans to oversee us.

So as their politicians are ugly, those that elect these vile things to oversee their land and self are as ugly, and vile also. <u>So, when your leaders do all to kill you, do not protest, sue, or complain to God. LIVE WITH THE SHIT YOU ELECTED TO OVERSEE YOU, YOUR LAND, AS WELL AS TAKE YOUR LIFE FROM YOU.</u>

Don't blame God or say, God do not care about you; humans. It is humans that truly do not care about self, God, the environment; land we live in; life on a whole.

<u>God did not elect demons to oversee anyone or kill anyone.</u> <u>You the people in society did this.</u> You wanted to lose your life thus, <u>you are losing your life.</u> <u>You have nothing to gain but death, and the Children of Death are literally killing you.</u>

As for my family, I am duly warning you. The person who is going to the dead; using obeah stop your shit. It is not warranted in life. Yes, I know the evils of some on my mother's side of the family, therefore, stop your shit lest you be consumed by death. Nastiness is not the way. Let those who have hurt you go, and truly look at the past sins of some that are in this family; the family some of us marry into from the past until now. Thus, some truly do not listen to good counsel. Some are covered under generational sins period. And I am going to leave it at that.

Dreamt snakes; these massive snakes that were about three times or more the size of Anacondas in water. Already know what this mean.

Now I am dreaming about the now President of the United States. I truly do not know if someone is going to try to assassinate him. Procession for me is death therefore, I am going to leave his dream alone. Man too demonic for my liking.

As for Africa I cannot remember my dream, but something is going to happen in Africa.

Is a land going to get decimated weather wise?

Yes, but which land is the question.

Michelle

BOOKS WRITTEN BY MICHELLE JEAN – 2020

FIRST BOOK OF 2020

BOOK TWO 2020

JUST ONE OF THOSE DAYS 2020

TRUTH – THE MONTH OF TRUTH – FEBRUARY 2020 AND BEYOND

ENGLAND – MANKIND

I DON'T KNOW BUT I DO

CANDIDLY SPEAKING LOVEY

THE COMPLEXITY OF LIFE – CONFUSION